FULL-TIME GAMBLER

♠ An American Classic ♣

—L. G. Holloway—

Fort Lee, New Jersey

To all the lovers of
the game...

Published by Barricade Books Inc.
185 Bridge Plaza North
Suite 308-A
Ft. Lee, NJ 07024

Printed in Canada.

First printing, second edition

PROEM

Many books on gambling have been written by professors, reformers, wishful thinkers, losers, and by operators who stay on the other side of the table. Their underlying message is: Don't play—or just play for fun—you can't win.

I am a full-time gambler and will show you how to grind out a steady profit. You don't need luck: luck is neither dependable nor permanent. What you need is winning knowledge, and you will find it in *this* book.

Would you stand out in the open in a battle zone and let your enemies take pot shots at you? It is no game with them; they are playing for keeps. Why commit financial suicide? The wise strategy is to get proper training, take protective measures, and have a plan for victory.

TABLE OF CONTENTS

PUBLISHER'S PREFACE

In the 1960s when Louis G. Holloway approached me with the idea of writing a book about his skills and experience, I was America's #1 skeptic.

He told me that he was a full-time gambler. His actual gaming occupied no more than an hour a day. But for several hours more, he would read every new booklet, pamphlet, system—everything that was published on the games he played.

Holloway explained that he was careful not to draw unnecessary attention because casinos were on the alert for card counters. He could pass as a Methodist minister and he played small.

He was satisfied to leave the tables with $50 or $75 for thirty or forty minutes of activity. He rarely gambled more than an hour a day.

"Show me," I said. And show me he did.

We spent several hours together each day for a week. We made forays at the blackjack tables. We made forays at the craps tables.

How did he show me?

Well, one morning at the Sands (the hot

place in town then and the casino that always comp'd me with an 18th floor penthouse) he invited me to sit with him at a blackjack table. We sat at opposite ends of the layout.

I watched him without seeming to. When Louis bet $5 or $10. I bet $50 or $100. When he went to $25, it was my signal that the deck was picture-rich and I went to $500.

I did marvelously well.

It was then that I made the decision to publish *Full-Time Gambler*.

It was one decision I've never regretted.

* * * *

Full-Time Gambler sold well. It went out of print shortly after Louis Holloway died.

Time had made some of the facts obsolete. New casinos rose from the desert sands. Old ones were imploded and it was as if they never existed. The City of Las Vegas exploded and soon you could walk from ancient Rome (Caesars Palace) to modern Paris (Paris) or from Venice (the Venetian) to Italy (the Bellagio). Perhaps you preferred to wander the streets of Manhattan (New York, New York).

In short, things changed.

Pressure increased for us to reissue this book. I resisted because there is now a flood of gaming books in the market place.

Even the book we published by Frank Renzoni, the man who brought baccarat to

America from Cuba was made obsolete by my own *Lyle Stuart on Baccarat*. To validate my credentials to write this one, I entered and won two major baccarat tournaments in Atlantic City to collect more than $250,000.

My *Casino Gambling for the Winner* was replaced nearly twenty years later by my *Winning at Casino Gambling*. The original had been cannibalized for years to provide material for gambling book writers who proclaimed their expertise while pirating my knowledge and philosophy.

No matter.

The question was, if I did reissue *Full-Time Gambler*, would I detract from its magic if I updated some of the facts in its pages. Today, for example, we know that savvy blackjack players would never fall for the insurance bet. Yet Holloway said to skip casinos "that do not even offer an insurance bet."

Holloway talks about standing on no less than "16" against a dealer's high card. That probably should have read "17." And of course, money values have changed. When he speaks of $20, you can translate it as $200 today.

* * * *

Louis Holloway once told me an interesting story. His son was a talented youth who was studying at Massachusetts Institute of Technology.

"Dad," the son said, "I know mathematics. There is no way anyone can overcome the odds against the player in a casino."

"Son," Holloway said, "This house we're in? That automobile outside? The food we eat? The money to pay your college tuition? Where did you think they all come from? It's all casino winnings!"

* * * *

I decided to resist the temptation to update or to add my later knowledge and wisdom to the pages that follow, because Holloway wrote what is now an American classic, and it should be read as such.

Lyle Stuart
August, 2001
Fort Lee, New Jersey

PERCENTAGE IS ENEMY
NUMBER ONE

If you think the Irish Sweepstakes is a good bet because scores of people win fortunes every year, or if you think keno is a good game because every week people win prizes up to $25,000, then you are a dreamer who ignores percentage. If you think a race player who bets every race and hits many longshots is smart, you are overlooking the fact that anything can get good temporarily, but anyone who constantly ignores the big "bite" is sure to get ground down.

Hunch and poor percentage players can get into winning streaks, but bookies and casino operators know the poor fools are just "living on borrowed time." If you hope to be a steady winner, you dare not ignore the percentage "bite." It takes determination and character to be a winner. To join the winning ranks, here's a good oath to say *and mean:* "I will never again make a bad percentage play."

What makes percentage so deadly is the compounding factor. At first glance it may seem like an unimportant thing, but the accumulated total can drown you. Few people realize how much

13

money they "turn over" in a short period of play. For example, the average players' "21" game shows about a 5 percent loss. Maybe they set aside a few hundred dollars for a weekend of speculation on their favorite game. If they bet just $1 or so per hand, hour after hour, they actually turn over hundreds or even thousands of dollars. Then that 5 percent compounded becomes a big chunk. After percentage has ground them down for a while, along comes a slump they can't weather, and the bankroll vanishes.

The players fighting against the very smallest possible percentage bite will survive longer and thus will have a better chance to catch a good upswing. You can fight giants if you are a fool, but you would have a better chance to win if you tackled a midget. If you were an army general attacking a fortified line, wouldn't you hit where the line was the weakest?

If you feel that confining your plays to the good percentage spots restricts your action too much, then you are like a spoiled child who insists on doing what he wants to do, even if it isn't good for him. You may be one of the sick ones psychiatrists talk about—a compulsive gambler. I get my kicks out of winning, not just making lots of bets. If you lack the control to pass the bad percentage plays, then you are not ready to join the winning ranks.

In horse racing, where the public determines

the odds, it is possible to find occasional bargains. In casino play, however, the odds are permanently set and only two kinds exist: Fair and Bad. The fair ones are where the percentage bite is very small. The bad ones are to be avoided like poison. Some are so bad I won't even waste space in this book explaining those games. You will merely be warned to pass them by.

The big wheels, slot machines, keno, bingo, and chuck-a-luck are games to be passed. Single-0 roulette, baccarat, and cleverly played "21" are fair games to tackle with the proper knowledge. Dice contains both good and bad bets, so know that game well before you jump in. The OK bets on a dice table are the *line bets, do* or *don't pass, do* or *don't come,* and *taking* or *laying* the odds on same. The percentage jumps way up on the center layout "propositions," field plays, place betting, Big 6 and 8, hardways, craps, etc., which I will explain shortly in the dice section.

DOWNSWINGS ARE DEADLY

All games of chance swing back and forth. Some people think these good and bad swings are "luck." They are perfectly normal and are part of the game, so it is your job to understand them fully. The house capitalizes on these swings to a tremendous advantage, and you must learn to do the same. Give this extremely important lesson plenty of time, thought, and research.

Losing players miscalculate the adverse effects and magnitude of downswings. Those who play bad percentage bets only hasten their disaster. The whole key to winning is to play a conservative game and outlast the bad runs, then play more boldly and cash out ahead on a good upswing.

Unfortunately, there is nothing regular about the back and forth or upswings and downswings of the game. We never know how long a run will last. All we know for sure is that there will be swings: little, big, or erratic. Even so, we *can* capitalize on this knowledge, as you will find later in this book.

The casino uses "table limits" to protect itself against a prolonged good swing in the player's direction. These limits also protect the house and doom the steep-progression players. Just as important as the house's limits should be the player's own personal capital limits. The player must apply a "stop-loss" to keep from losing everything in a prolonged downswing.

The house has infinitely more money than the player and can therefore weather the bad periods better than the individual customer. Anyone in the game on short capital is an almost certain loser, as the slightest downswing will knock him out. Mark this well: If you are on short capital, you shouldn't play. The educated professional with plenty of capital knows he has but little better than a 50–50 chance of winning. Mr. Nonprofessional with short capital has about one chance in a thousand. Knowing that your chance is this small, why try until you are properly equipped?

You may ask, "How bad can it get?" The answer is: "Worse than most people think." On the other hand, it can also get better than most people are prepared to accept or believe. Remember this important rule: Limit your losses, but don't limit your gains!

The majority of players think that swings of the game or runs of luck are the only thing that counts. Persons going to the races or to Nevada for a short time are easy victims for bad percentage plays; shortness of time and greed dominate

their judgment. Wild gambling and making lots
of bets will not produce proportionally more upswings. All you do is put more weight on the
downswings and you give Lady Luck very little
chance to catch you as you rush downhill. You
are like an athlete in a race agreeing to start
farther back of the line and pick up an added
weight burden. Would you step into the ring in
a championship fight and say, "Tie one hand behind my back, I can lick him anyway"?

It is your money and you can play any way
you like. The house will give you free drinks and
make you feel important while you make darned
fool bets. If they can get you loosened up and
away from the fair percentages over onto more
and more of the bad ones, they will beat you easier and quicker. The drinks you get at the table
are stronger than the ones you buy at the bar.

The lure of longshots is a temptation to resist
unless you fully understand the magnified swings
those plays encounter. The longer the odds, the
bigger the slumps and the more the capital
needed. Having consecutive losers alone isn't
necessarily the measure of a downswing. A
"bogged-down" period can be just as deadly,
even though it gets an occasional intermittent
winner.

LUCK AND THE LAW
OF AVERAGES

To say that winning is nothing but luck is pure nonsense. Luck and the law of averages are seldom around when you need them. Most players depend on luck and most players lose. If you ask a dealer or another player a good way to win, he will usually tell you one way is as good as another: It is all a matter of luck. You asked the wrong man; you asked a loser. The dictionary describes luck as a casual event or accident—either good or bad fortune. Do you expect to beat a tough game casually or accidentally?

You hear about big winners or you may see a drunk win a big pile. Is this really luck? Did you count how many losing players or losing drunks it took to produce each big winner? The situation would only be abnormal if there weren't some big winners and winning drunks once in a while.

If you were to do a study of ten million people going to the races and casinos over a period of time, you might find that about one-tenth of them came home winners each trip. On the second trip for those same people, you now only have one million to examine. On the third trip it is down to one hundred thousand; then down to ten thousand; and so on. Obviously some people will win several times in a row and start to think they are pretty smart. This isn't luck. It is perfectly normal. There are sure to be some poor players in the group not yet ground down.

On the other hand, if you find someone who has continued to win after scores of trips, months on end, you are no longer dealing in normal runs of luck. This rare individual is an educated, experienced full-time gambler. If you ask him, he will say luck has nothing to do with it. You might remember this: The man with the best knowledge has the best luck.

The law of averages will assert itself in projected time. Few players are aware it takes thousands of plays, and there is no law saying averages must assert themselves in the next dozen or so transactions. The races, wheels, dice, or cards can always just as easily get into deeper debt before they get better, so never count on the law of averages.

PLACES TO PLAY—
TIME TO PLAY

The time and place you play can be very important. On horse racing, the big major tracks are about the same, although handicapping methods should vary seasonally. At the medium and smaller tracks you get a little better break because you are not up against the smartest of players. In casino action the differences are more marked. By all means avoid the small, hungry, and illegal casinos. Casinos out on the "fringe" usually have gimmicks to attract customers. Beware of bargains; they are made back in other ways.

Always study the layouts and odds offered on casino tables. Also check their maximum and minimum bet limits. Look for the biggest range or spread. For example, one casino in downtown Las Vegas has a twenty-five-cent minimum on the dice line, but a limit of $1,000 for the maximum. This is a spread of 4,000 units—in an old casino that looks a little run-down. However, they are much better sports in that casino than in a very plush place out on the Strip that starts off at $1 and has a $200 maximum—a spread of a mere 200 units.

On some illegal casino layouts, and way-out Caribbean and European dice layouts, you will find "Cockeyes" barred instead of 2 or 12. The barring of a craps number is used to equalize the front and back line, and we will explain this in the dice section. The normal stand-off, or barring of a 2 or 12 on the *don't pass* or *don't come,* is altered to *bar three* in the "Cockeyed" places. This ups the percentage quite a bit against dice players, so avoid those places.

Don't get hooked on the difference between "to one" and "for one." When a layout says 7–1, this means 7-to-1: you get 7 plus your own 1. If it says 7-for-1, however, you get 6 plus your 1— a mighty big percent less! So be a little bit observing. On the game of "21," check those double-down rules, and also skip the places that do not even offer an insurance bet. Every little percentage point counts.

If roulette is your game, Europe is the best place to play. If dice is your game, stick to the bigger Nevada casinos. On "21" you get more single decks and uneducated dealers at Lake Tahoe than you do in Reno and Las Vegas in that order.

Casinos out of the United States have more restrictive betting limits. Some Caribbean spots have a $50 or $100 maximum. Plush places in the Bahamas may have a $5 minimum, and neither areas have a wide spread between minimum and maximum. Also be sure to check the layout offerings. On dice, for example, many have no "come" bet spots, forcing players to "place" their numbers—at a much bigger bite.

The time of day that you play should be determined by the attendance. Never play when it is just you and the shills. Although Nevada casinos stay open around the clock, the only busy hours are afternoons and evenings. Weekends are not the best time to play, especially in a peak season. Whenever the casinos are jammed, any kind of monkey business is less likely to be detected.

A good player is not appreciated when the casino is jammed full. The house figures it needs each seat or standing spot for a waiting list of suckers ready to drop their money swiftly.

Las Vegas is a bit too hot in the summer, unless you stay inside and only move around outside at night. Tahoe is ideal in summer, but a bit too jammed on weekends. Reno is both too hot and too cold, except in spring or fall. You will find race books in all three spots. A 10-percent tax is charged on all track betting. Racing Forms are free.

It helps if you rotate your action to many different places. You will find some places radiate a more friendly atmosphere. There is no reason to feel forced to patronize any one place. Stick to the places you like. There are scores to choose from. If a casino beats you a few times, there is no reason to accuse it of cheating. If a casino beats you continually, knock it off your list.

DEALERS AND CHEATING

Some dealers are nice; some are unpleasant; some are cheats; far too many are "wise guys." The dealer's life can get to be quite a bore. He sees so many foolish players he soon loses respect for all players. Dealers get so fast at money-handling and odds that they make the customers look like fumblers, and many dealers get the idea they are smarter than their patrons.

Most dealers are frustrated or cured losers who have become cynical. Very few of them try to understand cycles, patterns, or wagering plans. Dealers see nearly all system players lose, and this further convinces them that systems are no good. They fail to consider that most of the systems used against them are elementary, and that the users of those systems haven't much experience or research behind their play.

Pit bosses and box men are usually graduates from the dealer ranks. Some have financial interests in the casino. The main function of a pit boss is to keep the drinks and credit flowing to potentially big losers. Pit bosses are also supposed to remember good customers as well as watch for cheaters.

Cheating players, often called "crossroaders," indulge in card marking, dice switching, slot machine rigging, or anything else they can devise to steal some of the handy money. The house worries most about possible cooperation between a cheater and a dealer. Since the box take is watched, a dealer has to increase the theft from customers to pass over to a confederate. All winners are subject to closer scrutiny by the managers than are other players.

Your chances of being cheated in a major casino are minute. Cheating is more likely to occur in a card game than elsewhere. In any case, don't jump to conclusions or make false accusations. You are on the casino's property and need an unimpeachable witness. If you are convinced you have been cheated, write the Gaming Commission about it and make it a point to play somewhere else. It helps if you are not the biggest player at the table.

The casinos have many ways of getting rid of players they don't want. I call these "aggravation tactics," and I have had them used on me. For example, they can speed up the game and sweep away your chips, giving you an argument, and not giving you time for counting and calculations. Be ever watchful of how much you put down and where. Be firm when you are right, but don't lose your temper. The casinos need only the slightest excuse to order you out. Losing your temper also upsets your judgment. There are many forms of irritations and distractions. If you like liquor or have an eye for the girls, these diversions can be used to spoil your game.

Many race players are too quick to call a race crooked. The jockeys are always being accused of giving poor rides. Race players forget the fact that, when they win, some other players lose for the same reasons. It can help you as often as it hurts you. Crookedness in racing isn't a fraction of a percent and is infinitely less than people think. In any case, it can be turned to your advantage. Just watch that tote board for the hot ones.

At a dice table, if a big bettor is losing and is blaming crookedness, it is likely we would be playing a different game than his anyway, since we follow trends. If you think you have run up against a crooked card game, play somewhere else. Don't stay there trying to make your losses back where your mood is foul.

Only the High Rollers are considered dangerous to a casino. On my personal game I'm satisfied to grind out a moderate profit and keep moving around. Now and then, when I do hit a big winning, there are usually other big winners at the same table. If my winning comes on the dice back line, I may be the only one, as most players play the front line. The big difference between a good player and a poor one is what they do between big winnings. The poor players lose it all back. You get a thrill and a minor form of intoxication from a big winning. It is important that you continue to handle your money wisely even when you are drunk with success.

Some players think they have to tip the dealers any time they get a big payoff. Actually they cannot afford this constant bite out of their winnings. The only time to tip is when you are *quitting* winners. Dealers will flatter and pamper good tippers. A little tip is OK for good will, but only when you are quitting ahead for the session.

DICE

As played in Nevada, dice offers the lowest negative percentage to the smart bettors. This applies only to those who concentrate on the *line bets, do* or *don't pass, come* or *don't come,* and the *taking* or *laying* of odds on those established points. The negative percentage of −1.4 is cut to half that much when one takes odds for a similar amount of money, as the odds are "free." In the "laying" of odds, where you put up more than your bet size, the "free" part makes the negative percentage even less than half the −1.4. This should tell you why the "don't" bettors get a wee bit the best of it.

In a private game where there is no "bar" number on the *don't,* they definitely have an edge. Dice, as played in legal casinos, always has a bar number. Thus there is no such thing as betting with or against the house. In the Reno-Tahoe area of Nevada the *two* is barred; in the Las Vegas area, the *twelve* is barred. It's the same percentage—just a minor difference in the layouts.

29

Layout

The dice layouts differ in each club, although the payoffs and meanings are standardized. In the Tahoe-Reno area the *don't pass* is located behind the field and, if a point is thrown, the dealer will move your money behind the box of that number. In Las Vegas, the *don't* line is directly behind the *do pass* line and they leave your money there until the transaction is completed. A dice player soon adapts to the minor differences in layouts. Good players keep their eyes on their money and see that they get the proper even-money payoffs plus odds. At a crowded table, when lots of participants are playing *place bets* and *come* bets for all different amounts and odds, it can get confusing and it helps to know all of your bets accurately.

Outside of Nevada many layouts do not have *come* betting, forcing all persons interested in numbers to play *place*. Usually this is done for a 5 percent fee. In some instances this is better than the Nevada offering. However, we do not advise *place,* as it is a bad percentage: —1.4 is rough enough; 5 percent is too much; 10 percent is outrageous.

From the Chances and Odds Table we learn many things of importance. All single throw or "on-the-hop" bets and center layout plays are

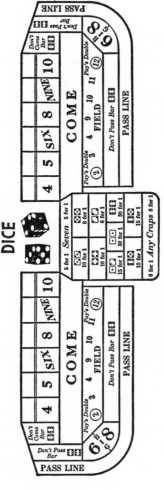

Typical Las Vegas Strip Bank Craps Layout

Pass line bets are always outer rim nearest the players.
Don't pass (Bar 12) is directly behind *pass* in Las Vegas area.
Come bets are large separate area.
Don't come bets layout area and handling differ by casinos.
Field bets clearly marked. Prefer layouts that pay triple on 12's.
Main difference between casinos is found in their center layouts.

Holloway's Chances and Odds Table

NUMBER or Throw	WAYS It Can Be Thrown	RATIO of Chances	CORRECT ODDS Should Be	ACTUAL ODDS Paid	PERCENT LOSS
2	1 way, 1-1	1/36th	35–1	30–1	–14
3	2 ways, 1-2,2-1	1/18th	17–1	15–1	–11
4	3 ways, 1-3,3-1,2-2	1/12th	11–1	9–1	–17
5	4 ways, 1-4,4-1,2-3,3-2	1/9th	8–1	7–1	–11
6	5 ways, 1-5,5-1,2-4,4-2,3-3	5/36ths	6.2–1	5–1	–17
7	6 ways, 1-6,6-1,2-5,5-2,3-4,4-3	1/6th	5–1	4–1	–20
8	5 ways, 2-6,6-2,3-5,5-3,4-4	5/36ths	6.2–1	5–1	–17
9	4 ways, 3-6,6-3,4-5,5-4	1/9th	8–1	7–1	–11
10	3 ways, 4-6,6-4,5-5	1/12th	11–1	9–1	–17
11	2 ways, 5-6,6-5	1/18th	17–1	15–1	–11
12	1 way, 6-6	1/36th	35–1	30–1	–14
Hop Hard Way	1 way, paired, one throw only	1/36th	35–1	30–1	–14
Hardway 4 or 10	1 way, before a 7 or easy way	1/9th	8–1	7–1	–11
Hardway 6 or 8	1 way, before a 7 or easy way	1/11th	10–1	9–1	– 9

Bet	Ways				
Any Craps	4 ways, 1-1-2,2-1,6-6		8-1	7-1	−11
Horn Bet	6 ways, craps plus eleven; *Varies		5-1	4-1	−20
Field Bet	16 ways, 2,3,4,9,10,11,12; †Varies	4/9ths	5-4	1-1	− 7.5
Big 6 or Big 8	5 ways each before a 7 out	5/11ths	6-5	1-1	−17
Place 4 or 10	3 ways each before a 7 out	1/3rd	2-1	9-5	−10
Place 5 or 9	4 ways each before a 7 out	2/5ths	3-2	7-5	− 7.5
Place 6 or 8	5 ways each before a 7 out	5/11ths	6-5	7-6	− 2.8
Taking Odds 4 or 10	3 ways each before a 7 out	1/3rd	2-1	2-1	0
Taking Odds 5 or 9	4 ways each before a 7 out	2/5ths	3-2	3-2	0
Taking Odds 6 or 8	5 ways each before a 7 out	5/11ths	6-5	6-5	0
Laying Odds 4 or 10	6 ways on 7 before 3 ways	2-1	1-2	1-2	0
Laying Odds 5 or 9	6 ways on 7 before 4 ways	3-2	2-3	2-3	0
Laying Odds 6 or 8	6 ways on 7 before 5 ways	6-5	5-6	5-6	0

* Horn bets sometimes paid separately.   † Field bets boosted by specials on 2 and 12.

very bad percentage bets. The Big 6 and Big 8 bets are not in the center, but they also are very foolish. If you like a 6 or 8 after the point is established, come up with 6 units and make it a *place* bet, getting 7–6 odds, which isn't too bad. Other *place* bets are worse and should be avoided.

Before a point is established, the *pass* or *don't pass lines* have a pinch less than 50 percent chance of paying even money. The *don't pass* is above 50 percent, but the 3 percent of the time a bar number comes in kills its advantage. After a point is established, the 7 is the most likely. For this reason the house will permit a new and uninformed player to bet the *pass line* any time. You can't take your money off the *pass line* once you put it down, but you can take off odds or a back line at any time. It is foolish to refuse a back line number or take your money off once you have an edge.

Explanation of the Game

The dice tables would get much more business if a bigger effort was made to explain the games in the casinos. Fifty percent of the business in Nevada comes from tourists there for the first or second time, and the dice table puzzles them completely. They see players betting money all over the place in all different amounts and getting all kinds of payoffs.

A few spots have short teaching sessions, and some of the tables have a sign "Instructions Table," where you can ask the dealer questions. Many people are embarrassed to show their ignorance, and often the dealers' explanations only add to the confusion. I have listened in at the Instructions Tables on occasions, and those where the game is not in progress do give satisfactory explanations. However, you can be sure they *do not* tell people the losing percentages or which are good bets and which are bad. If the more advanced students will forgive the digression, we must take time out to explain each game properly.

Technically speaking, a dice game starts over with each new "come out roll." Players already at the table may be involved in some bets that are not cleared since the last "come out," and, of course, the systematic players are also involved in wagering plans, but we must start explaining from the official "come out."

The dice are passed to a shooter. Each person is given a turn at shooting. He can pass the dice and not shoot if he prefers. A shooter holds the dice until he "7's out" or fails to make a point.

On the first roll, if the shooter throws a 7 or 11, this is a "natural" pass; the *pass line* wins, the *don't pass line* loses. If, on the other hand, on the first roll, the shooter throws a "craps" number, 2,3, or 12, the *pass line* loses, the *don't pass line* (or back line) wins. However, if the craps number is a bar number,* the *pass line* still loses, but the back line does *not* win; they have a stand-off. If the shooter does not throw a natural or a craps, then he throws a "point." This is the main point. The dealers then place a marker on that point number so all will know. Points are 4,5,6,8,9,10.

After the shooter has rolled a point, he continues to toss the dice until he either makes the point or throws a 7. If he makes the point, this, again, is a completed pass; the front line wins, the back line loses. If, however, he "7's out," then the *pass line* loses and the back line or *don't pass* wins.

Meantime, after the official *come out,* all sorts of other betting goes on. This is what is so confusing to a beginner. The amusing part is that the beginner would actually be better off if *passes* and *don't passes* were all he *ever* learned about the game. But you just about have to know all the rest to keep up with what's going on and to keep from being considered stupid.

The center layout plays (single throw bets) can be made any time on any roll. None of these is a good bet (see Chances and Odds Table). To

---

* Remember, the bar number can differ on casino layouts.

bet a single throw play, the dealers prefer that you toss in the right amount of money and tell them in a loud, clear voice what it is you want. They have ways of locating and stacking the money so they know who to pay if it wins. They place each bet in the general direction of the player, and often at a crowded table they have to be real wizards to remember who gets what and avoid arguments. We will discuss each separate bet but, for now, let's get back to the main issue; that is, *line bets.*

Line Bets

When you place your money on the *pass line* or the *don't pass line* on the *come out* roll, you are making an *even money* bet. You either lose or get back your own bet plus one payoff of the same amount. Your chances of success are not quite 50–50, the wee pinch of house percentage amounts to —1.4 percent.

There is no such thing as "betting with the house," as some people think they are doing when they play the back line or *don't pass.* The house extracts a nearly equal percentage from either line. It is true, however, that the majority of the players bet the dice *do pass,* and usually that line is played much more than the back line. For this reason a table is considered "cold" if the dice are not passing.

It has always amused me to hear a bettor complain when the back line is in a prolonged good run. Nobody is twisting his arm forcing him to stay on the *pass line*. The back line runs can be just as frequent and just as long as the front line runs. Don't limit your thinking.

Possibly one of the stronger appeals of the front line over the back line is the "taking of odds." You can put up less and get paid more. Of course, the chances are proportional; this is no real advantage.

Line Bet Odds

Once a point is established, you are now offered an opportunity to take or lay *free odds*. This is a bargain percentagewise, since all other bets in the casino have a "take" or bite. Again, consult the Chances and Odds Table. You will note that on a point of 4 or 10, it is 2–1 against the shooter making that point, meaning a 7 is now twice as likely as either a 4 or a 10. If you already had a bet on the *pass line,* you can now place a like amount of money "at odds." If the point 4 or 10 wins, you get even money for your *line bet,* and 2–1 for your odds bet. The 4's and 10's are obviously the toughest points to make: They are farthest out from a 7, which hits the most frequently.

If your bet was on the *don't pass* (or back

line) and the shooter's point is 4 or 10, the reverse odds now apply. In this case, you have a
better chance of winning now than does the *pass
line;* therefore you must accept shorter odds, or
"odds-on" prices. This is like betting a favorite to
show. On the back line, if you wish to "lay odds"
on your bet, you must know the proper odds and
give the dealer the proper amount. On a 4 or 10,
you put up twice as much as your bet to win an
additional unit. For example, if you had bet $1
on a back line and the point was 4 or 10, you
put up 2 more. If you win your bet and a 7
comes up before the point, you win your 1, plus
1 more, then you get your 2 back, plus 1 more
for that.

On line points, it is vital that you know your
proper odds and bet the right amount. On a
point of 4 or 10, it is easy. If, however, the line
point is 5 or 9, you cannot get proper odds unless your bet is in multiples of two. If you have
a bet on the line and a 5 or a 9 becomes the
point, in order to take odds, your bet should be
2 units on the line, or 4 units, or 6, or 8, etc. The
reason is this: The odds on a 5 or a 9 are 3–2.
For each 2 you put down you get back a profit of
3 if the shooter makes the point. On the back
line, again the situation is reversed: Now you
have to put up 3 for each 2 you have bet. In
some of the cheaper casinos, where they break
to the half dollar or use quarters, you can bet $1

and still get proper odds on a 5 or 9, because actually you are betting *two* half dollars.

You see many foolish things at a crap table. Some players, playing on the Las Vegas Strip, for example, where they break to the dollar, will get a point of 5,6,8, or 9, when they have a dollar bet. They then proceed to put $1 down behind that bet for odds. The dealers usually say nothing, but all experienced crapshooters know they are taking an awful percentage bite on that wasted dollar. All they will win is even money, and at poor odds to do so. This is why I repeat, "you must know proper odds."

If the shooter's point is a 6 or an 8, now it takes multiples of 5 to get proper odds. If you have a 5 on the line for a point of 6 or 8, you can put down another 5 and get 6 for it if the shooter makes the point. If your 5-unit bet was on the back line, you now have to put up 6 at laying odds to make another 5. So, once and for all, know the odds on the three sets of points. The 4's and 10's are alike, the 5's and 9's are alike, and the 6's and 8's are treated the same. Always try to bet at least 2 units, then you can at least take odds or lay odds on 4's, 5's, 9's, and 10's. If you bet a 5-unit minimum, you can still take odds on the 5's and 9's for 4 units' worth. Now get this: The taking of odds can be done for *less* than your *line bet,* but not *more.* There are a few exceptional places that will permit "double odds" taking. These are little fringe places dealing in smaller players usually.

Finally, on the subject of taking or laying odds, it *is* advised. But there is one disconcerting thought on the subject, which I will discuss later under wagering: It takes more capital and magnifies the swings.

Come Bets

Some beginners stepping up to a dice table think the "come" bet area means they can play on the point number to come up. It doesn't mean this at all. The proper name for "come" betting should be "new point" or "fresh start," but that might be even more confusing.

Actually, "come" betting is just exactly like *line betting,* except that you can start at any time. If the shooter has an established point, you don't have to wait for that point to be made or missed. If you put a bet out on the "come," you now take the consequences of the very next roll. If it is a 7 or 11, you win; if it is a craps number, you lose. If it is a point number, your *come* money is now moved by the dealer up to the numbers boxes on the layout. The dealer positions the *come* money in such a way that he knows who placed the *come* bet. If the shooter hits a 7 after your *come* money has been moved, you lose at the same time the *line bets* also

"7-out." Thus, all *come* money is cleared on any miss-out. However, if the shooter makes his point, your *come* action is still not a completed transaction until you again make your *come* point. Also, if the shooter goes on to new points and new passes, still with no intervening 7, your *come* bet still goes on separately until its own point shows.

The *come* betting can get a little confusing and somewhat "uncontrollable," and it is difficult to adapt to a wagering plan. For example, you can play the *come* on every roll (except a new official *come-out*), and eventually have *come* money on all the numbers. You can be collecting some, replacing them, taking odds on them, and changing money so fast you hardly know whether you are coming or going. A table that is loaded with *come* bets is a busy table, until there is a 7, then a big groan comes from the players and the whole thing starts all over again. A *come* bet is not like a *place* bet, even though the dealer puts the money in the number box area. The *place* bets and the *don't come* bets are located a little differently. Usually *come* is the front part of the number box, *place* is in the center, and *don't come* is behind. You'll get onto that in short order after watching a table a while.

"Don't come" betting is like "don't pass," again with the difference that it can be placed at any time. You can take odds on *come* bets and lay odds on *don't come* bets, just as you do on the *pass* and *don't pass* lines. Some casinos outside of the United States do not have areas for *come* bets, forcing the players who want more numbers to "place" them, which is a bigger percentage bite. Wherever you play, be sure to study the layout and rules.

Pass line betting, taking odds, then *come* betting and taking odds is the most common or typical High Roller's game. It is a good game percentagewise provided that the player does not additionally buy numbers and throw in any craps, 11's, and hardway bets, as some do. This is a very fast and busy crap game. Players of this type do fine when the shooter takes a long time to make his point or 7-out. Where there are lots of intervening numbers, it is called a *long come hand*. Just one 7 and all transactions are terminated.

Actually a *come* player is playing a game of 7's and should study the cycle on 7's. The frequency of 7's determines his whole game. They may make one, or two, or three *come* numbers before being knocked off by a 7. Then again, they can go a big string. Their bankroll goes up and down so fast that they play a rather poorly organized game. For example, a shooter could come out with a point, and the player has a line bet, then takes odds. Then the shooter makes all of the other points, and the player again bets them all and takes odds on all. I have seen it happen hundreds of times, when the entire number box will be loaded with *come* numbers, making a dozen bets per player (including odds bets), and then the entire lot will be wiped out by a 7 before a single number was made.

I don't particularly care for this type of game, as I am involved in systematic wagering and the study of cycles and patterns. A good *come* player, however, can win a lot or lose a lot quickly and, if he has mastered the "quit ahead" technique, he can do all right for quite a few sessions. Nevertheless, there is always a prolonged downbeat for this kind of game that eventually hits, and it is a bit worse than on straight line play because of the magnified swings.

Place Betting

The numbers box on the dice table shows the point numbers, 4,5,6,8,9,10. Any of these numbers may be played "place" at any time. If you *place* a number, you are betting it will come up before a 7. If a 7 comes, you lose. *Place* bets do not pay true odds, and they are not good percentage plays. With eastern style craps (different from bank craps), you can "buy" the *place* numbers for a fee of 5 percent of your bet, and then get true odds. Still no good percentagewise.

Some people at a dice table have to have more action than the *line bets*. You see this same "bet crazy" fever at a "21" table when players split *every* pair they get, just to play more hands. On a roulette table, these players cover nearly every number on the board at every spin. I'll bet that when they go through a cafeteria line they put three times as much on their trays as they can eat.

If you *must place* a number, be sure to give the dealer the proper amount. To *place* the 6 or 8, you put up 6 units to get back 7. The house pays you 7–6 odds. These two numbers are the best *place* numbers with the smallest bite. To *place* a 5 or 9, the house pays 7–5; you should bet 5 units. To *place* a 4 or 10, they pay 9–5; again hand in 5 units.

Some crazy players who want to *place* a number will put up one unit. Some dealers will take it and say nothing, paying *even money* if the number wins. It is bad enough to see people play the Big 6 and Big 8 at 17 percent loss. We professionals stand there fighting against −1.4, and up comes some nut giving away 17 or more! It doesn't pay to say anything to the uninformed players, as they usually resent your advice at the table. Players like that don't last long; they are gone in five or ten minutes.

Field Betting

You might call the *field* a typical beginner's bet. It is easy to reach, it doesn't take much understanding, you get a lot of numbers and action on every roll. Field betting isn't too bad in areas where they pay triple on the 12's. In other spots the loss is 5 percent and more, so stay out of the field. (That's for the cows.) With numbers 2,3,4,9,10,11,12 going for you it looks good, just like keno.

Playing the Hardways

Whenever a point number is an even number, such as 4,6,8, or 10, most players will also bet it to come in the "hardway" or in a pair. A hardway bet can be made at any time on any even number. The bet stands until a 7 comes along or that same number is thrown the "easy" way, meaning nonpairing. Hardways are probably the most popular longshots on the dice table.

The odds on a hardway 6 or 8 are better than those on 4's or 10's. This is because more *easy* 6's and 8's can be made, killing the bet. If a shooter makes his point, the hardways are still in action until they either win, lose, or the player takes them off. Most players declare their hardway bets "off on the come-out roll." Those who consider all rolls alike will let them stand.

It is wise to know if your hardway and *place* bets are "off" or "going" on the *come-out* roll, so there is no argument with the dealer. Declare your intentions. (My declaration is: Don't play the hardways.) The Chances and Odds Table will show you the large negative percentage on center layout bets. The house loves all players who cover the hardways. It is a tough fight against −1.4 percent, and anyone exposing his money to bigger bites is asking to be ground down quicker. Temporary success notwithstanding, hardways are strictly money-grinders for the house, not the player.

Dice Longshots

The 2's and 12's are also "hardways" that can only be won one way—in a pair. The 2's and 12's do *not* stay up until a 7 comes along however: They are longshot one-roll plays. Instead of paying 35–1 as they should, they pay only 30–1. Some houses only pay 30-for-1. Very bad percentages on those longshots, so pass them. The 3's and 11's are popular bets, especially the 11's. Where they should pay 17–1 they usually pay only 15–1 (except in gyp houses at 15-for-1), and again these are tempting odds . . . but you must learn to resist temptations.

The "on the hop" one-roll pairs are similar to bets on 2's or 12's and offer the same poor percentage. The "horn" bet encompasses 2,3,11, and 12. Most places require a 4-unit bet and will pay whichever of the horn numbers comes in. Other places pay the horn at one fixed price. In any case take the Panama Canal and skip the horn; it will scuttle your bankroll quickly.

Some shooters seem to think that, if they make a bet on the *pass line,* it is then wise to protect their bet against loss by a bet on "any craps." If you bet every horse in a race with a bookmaker, he'd have a big smile of happiness because he gets his percentage bite out of every bet you make. Thus the temporary "protection" the crapshooter takes on the first throw is only exposing more of his money at a bigger percentage. "Any craps" is a very popular bet on the dice table but, if you will again check the Chances and Odds Table to see the percentage loss on such a play, you'll see why I *do not* advise "any craps."

Once a point is established, some dice players get worried about a 7 coming in. They, too, think they are protecting their *line bet* by betting on the 7 specifically in the center layout. The house will give you all the free drinks you can drink if you will just go on thinking like that (and paying them 17 percent on every dollar you invest). The 7 should pay 5–1, but it only pays 4–1.

As I have explained the possible dice bets, and advised against most, you may be wondering *when* this book is going to tell *what to play to win*. This advice will come under cycles, patterns, wagering plans, *and* total knowledge application, so please be patient. Get your basic facts straight first. On all the games, you *must* know good bets from bad, and know why you must stick to the low-percentage spots. Then, and not until then, are you ready for money management, capital division, pushing the good runs, and many more things.

There is no shortcut to complete knowledge. A good fighter reacts properly with trained reflexes; he protects himself as best he can and conserves his energy (or betting money) to use at the proper time. People are too anxious to win and they want a simple little trick so they can rush out and kill the giant. Maybe you are capable of specializing on *one* simple winning thing, which is an OK way to win, but it sure helps if you know right from wrong on all other things so you don't get tempted while waiting for your specialized play to come up.

ROULETTE

This game has a dignity and studious atmosphere that differs from other casino games. Roulette players are more concerned with their systems dealing in mathematical wagering and sequences. They appreciate a chance to sit down away from the excited cries at the dice table or the incessant spieling of the dealers. The roulette player is not concerned with the necessity of constant decisions as in a card game, nor is he affected by what the other players may do. The true roulette player plays his game far better and lasts longer than other speculators.

The player starts his game by "buying in" with colored chips. Each player gets a different color. American style, the minimum purchase is one stack. You can buy as many stacks, at any value, at any time as you like.

Each table has its maximum and minimum. The lowest value is 10¢ chips, $2 a stack. On the Las Vegas Strip, some casinos do not sell lower than 25¢ chips; some start at 50¢. Maximum bet on a single number (known as "straight up") is $10 in cheaper places, and goes up to about $25 in better ones. Limits can

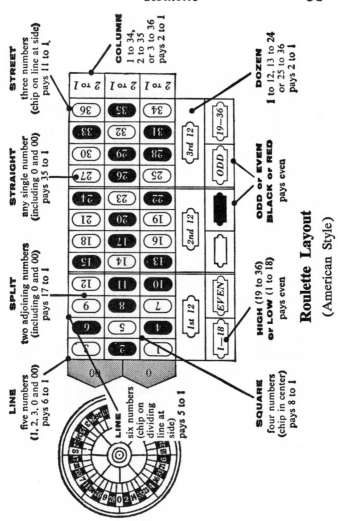

Roulette Layout
(American Style)

STREET
three numbers
(chip on line at side)
pays 11 to 1.

COLUMN
1 to 34,
2 to 35
or 3 to 36
pays 2 to 1

DOZEN
1 to 12, 13 to 24
or 25 to 36
pays 2 to 1

STRAIGHT
any single number
(including 0 and 00)
pays 35 to 1

ODD or EVEN
BLACK or RED
pays even

SPLIT
two adjoining numbers
(including 0 and 00)
pays 17 to 1

HIGH (19 to 36)
or LOW (1 to 18)
pays even

LINE
five numbers
(1, 2, 3, 0 and 00)
pays 6 to 1

SQUARE
four numbers
(chip in center)
pays 8 to 1

LINE
six numbers
(chip on
dividing
line at
side)
pays 5 to 1

be removed or raised for special customers on request. The minimum bets on "outside" combination bets, such as even money or 2–1 bets, usually start at 25¢ in the cheaper places, and are usually $1 in the more expensive ones. Maximum bets on the "outside" range from $100 up to $500. A few go to $1,000. Be sure to know limits wherever you play.

Roulette systems are in two parts. Both the method of selection and the method of wagering must be properly combined. It is advisable to practice a little (with inexpensive chips or on a home toy wheel) in order to get your two-phase system working smoothly. The actual play "under fire" can be tougher than paperwork. It is easy to get "rattled" and make costly mistakes. When you get confused you may have to break off the action with a loss.

The most common (and most worthless) method of selection is the "scattercash" or hunch method. Players using this method usually buy a few stacks of chips and scatter them all over the board. Naturally they hit some winners, and the dealer pushes them a big pile of chips. Since they had one-third or more, sometimes as much as two-thirds or three-fourths of the board covered, it doesn't make them smart or lucky to cash winners. But somehow the excitement of getting all those cute colored chips to scatter around carries them away. The game swings back and forth. Their pile may get bigger and bigger—*for a while*. What they are actually doing is exposing scores and scores of chips all over the place to the adverse percentage and, sure enough, it doesn't take long to clean them out.

Roulette offers many different kinds of bets. (See Layout for explanations.) You place your chips wherever you wish. If you are out of reach of a distant number or spot, the dealer will place it for you. Through different placements or combinations, the roulette player can get almost any odds. If he wants less than even money, he can cover two dozens or two columns at the same time. This would cost two (outside) chips, and bring a return of three if either dozen won. Thus 1–2 odds.

There are three different kinds of 1–1 or even-money-odds bets: the red or black, the high or low, and the odd or even. Then there are two different kinds of 2–1 bets, six placements in all, on the 2–1 dozens (one-third of the board at a time). To get 3–1, the player can let an even money bet ride twice. For other odds, clear up to 35–1, see Layout. System possibilities are unlimited.

In Reno, the Nevada Club on Virginia Street offers single-0 roulette. It has thrived and survived for years with this smaller percentage going for the house (European style). One number out of 37, or a percentage of —2.7 against the player, makes the Nevada Club the best place for roulette system players.

The other wheels in the state are more greedy. They have single with double-00's or 2/38ths (—5.26 percent) against the player. As a roulette fan myself, I'd like to see roulette make a comeback in this country, and it might have a chance if the clubs made it a better game. The clubs, however, figure the tourists do not pay attention to percentages and they might as well take a bigger bite. The —5.26 percent makes Nevada roulette a tough game to beat. Even so, it can be done *if* you put forth a serious effort. This means sufficient knowledge, understanding, patience, *and* capital. To become a successful professional gambler is a very difficult undertaking. Nevertheless it is a worthy challenge. You will know you have been in a fight, and when you beat the tough old tiger your glow will be contentment as well as prosperity. Gambling need not be a dull, boring, idle pastime.

In systematic gambling, there are two main schools of thought. One is what we call the "maturity of chances," or trying to collect on something that is "overdue" to hit. This one is followed by the believers in the "law of averages."

The other approach, which I personally

favor, is the "immaturity of chances," or going in the direction of that kind of play that is *hitting now:* in other words, trying to get in on the current hot runs. There is no certainty that a good run will continue, or that a bad run will terminate. However I *do* base my play on years of experience and research.

Beware the pitfall we call "peak picking." Too many horseplayers and gaming system players do a little checking until they find something that looks good, then, without lengthy further checking, "off to the races" they go, only to find later that the system rules did nothing more than point to a coincidental high peak.

The player who picks one type of bet and sticks to it, on a *conservative* wagering plan, will last longer than the typical weak and aimless player who changes ideas constantly whenever the method he is playing hits a little slump. The fear of loss must be overcome. The casinos wouldn't stay in business very long if they got scared every time a player won a little. If you are on short capital, *don't play.* Or, at least go to very inexpensive tables where your smaller capital will be adequate for your plan. Remember, it is a tough game. You can't afford to put unnecessary hazards in your way.

I think you will find that a big improvement on the "overdue" method is to wait out a slump and start on your pet plan *after* it hits. Many times at a roulette table I have seen players stick with one number or section through painfully long slumps. Some don't make it through. Then, when they quit, the number will start hitting. In your research, give thought to a "slump breaker." (See section on "Wagering.")

"21"

The game of "21," or blackjack, is one of the most popular, if not *the* most popular, in Nevada. The smart player has an excellent chance of coming close to breaking even with a good strategy, and he can break into some good winning runs. The card counter can actually find an occasional bargain and make a little money. This challenge to the intelligence of the players draws quite a following. Unfortunately, 95 percent of the players do *not* use good strategies and 99 percent of them are incapable of card counting at the speed of the game.

Owing to the publicity given to many books and incidents of big winners, the clubs are alerted to card counters and have many anti-counter measures. Some casinos use multiple decks dealt out of a box; some use multiple decks dealt face up; some casinos shuffle too frequently; and some casinos use the "down grab," which does not permit the player to see many cards other than his own and the dealer's. Casinos using multiple decks figure this lessens the value of card counting, and even those places shuffle before the decks are run through.

View of "21" Table from the Player's Side

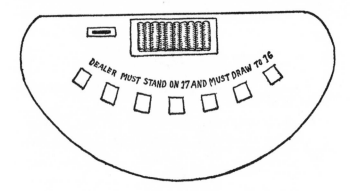

DEALER MUST STAND ON 17 AND MUST DRAW TO 16

The players sit on stools and put their bet amount on the little square marks nearest them. One player can play more than one hand unless the table is crowded. The bet must be made before the deal. After the player gets his first two cards, he decides if he has a satisfactory score or wants additional cards. If he has "21" on the first two cards, he turns his cards face up immediately and gets paid off at 1½–1 (or 3–2) odds. If he wants to draw more cards, he gets his chance when his turn comes in rotation. The dealer draws last. If the player goes over 21, he cannot draw more cards and he "tosses in" his cards. If he does not go over 21, general procedure is to slip the cards under the bet money, which indicates the player will "stand" on the cards he has. After all the players have gone broke or made their stand, the dealer turns his cards up and completes his drawing according to the stated rules: Stand on 17 (or more), draw to 16 (or less). At this point, the dealer either pays or collects.

The majority of "21" players lose for reasons other than strategy. They have insufficient capital to weather bad streaks, or they follow hunches, or they do a poor job of card counting. Some players actually think card counting amounts to watching the last few cards and, if a lot of big ones just went by, the next one should be small, or vice versa.

Too many players think blackjack is a very simple game and the player has almost as good a chance as the dealer. IF you go by the same rules as the dealer (hit 16, stand on 17), or if you go by a rule like "never hit a breaking hand," this is a very poor strategy; you will lose several percentage points on the dollar. A flat play loss of several percentage points will grind you down very swiftly in spite of temporary lucky runs.

The house edge in "21" comes mainly from the fact that the dealer goes broke last and takes all ties when you both go broke. Edges of lesser importance are things like players constantly having to make decisions, and the players not being able to bet on the dealer when he is in a good run. (In dice, for example, or roulette-red-and-black, you can bet either way the hot run is going.)

Another factor in the house's favor is the table limit. Any limitation placed on your wagering hampers your recovery from slumps. By all means check table limits, especially in small places, before you start to play.

As an illustration of the "limited logic" of the "21" players, the house offers and sells a lot of "insurance." This type of special bet is offered in Las Vegas and at Lake Tahoe. Not all places in Reno offer the insurance bet, but some do. This is separate from your own hand, a special proposition whenever the dealer has an ace for his up card. You are offered 2–1 odds if you wish to bet that he has a 10-count card down, thus making his hand a "blackjack." If he has a "natural 21" you will lose (unless you also have a 2-card 21 count). You are permitted to bet up to one-half of the amount you have on your regular bet. For example, if you had two chips bet, and the dealer turned up with an ace showing, you could bet one chip on 2–1 insurance. Then if he has blackjack, you get 2–1 on your insurance bet, thus not losing the amount of your regular bet.

The house explains to the player that "insurance" is a good bet if the player has a good hand, especially if the player has a blackjack of his own, for, according to the house, then the player "can't lose"; he is a cinch to break even or win. If you fail to reason through the "insurance gimmick," you are not ready to be a good "21" player. It is surprising how many arguments you can get into, even with dealers and pit bosses on the logic or fallacy of insurance. Let us examine the facts.

Insurance does not concern what you have in your hand; it is merely a bet on what the dealer has in his hand. Thus you are not insuring your hand at all; insurance should be considered separately. The dealer has an ace up. There are 13 denominations of cards: aces, 2's, 3's, 4's, 5's, 6's, 7's, 8's, 9's, 10's, jacks, queens, and kings. The 10's, jacks, queens, and kings are four denominations in number, against ace through 9's, *nine* of a kind that cannot make blackjack. Thus the normal ratio is not 4-to-8, but 4-to-9 (less one known ace). In a full deck, then, if the dealer had two cards and you had two cards, that's 48 cards remaining. Let's say you haven't looked at your cards, for it doesn't matter too much anyway. We would know then that, of 52 cards, only the ace is known, 51 cards left. Of those 51, there are 16 possible 10-counters, one of which the dealer needs to make a blackjack. Against those 16, there are 35 of the nonblackjacking kind. 16–35—is not true odds. If it was 16–32 —that would be a true ratio.

My point is that the aces (3/51sts) are the percentage against you—almost 6 percent going for the house on insurance bets. It matters not if you "save" or "cinch" your bet on one hand. Every time you shove your money out on the insurance line at 2–1, you are getting 6 percent less than you should, so don't take insurance under normal circumstances.

Card counting can change the whole picture. Suppose you kept track of the large and small cards that were gone and knew what remained in the deck. Suppose, for example, 20 cards were left unknown (including the one the dealer has down). Your count indicated there were 10 small cards and 10 big cards left. (Big cards mean 10's, jacks, queens, and kings.) This would be a 50–50 ratio, or an even money chance the dealer would turn up a blackjack. Now at 2–1, insurance would be a beautiful bargain! That kind of profit on your money is rarely offered in a gambling casino, so *grab it quick!*

I was amused at the stupidity of a dealer one day when he asked me, "How come you didn't insure your blackjack a while ago, and now you take insurance when you have a lousy hand?"

I didn't bother to explain to him that what I had in my hand didn't matter, it was *his* hand I was betting my insurance on. Instead I let him think I was just another nutty player.

Before we go deeper into card counting, let's settle on a good strategy. You can take my word that this strategy is computer and scientifically proved. It is not quite good enough to beat the dealer's edge, but it is good enough to use without card counting and to use in a multiple deck game and not take a big percentage loss. This is what we call a normal strategy; you must use it and not hunches unless you do card count and know when to alter the strategy. This "normal strategy" is also advised so you can concentrate on money management and pay attention to your winning and losing streaks, which are also very important to winning at any game of chance.

When dealer has 2 or 3 (up) showing, stand on 13 (or more) in your hand and take no more "hits." When dealer has 4,5, or 6 showing, stand on 12; otherwise stand on 17. If your hand is "soft," which includes an ace, draw to a 17, but stand on 18. (An ace counts as 1 or 11.) Regarding splitting pairs, it is OK to split 8's or aces, but do not split 4's, 5's, 6's, 9's or 10's. If your card count is 10 or 11, it is OK to "double down" and take one card for double your bet.

Please note, the doubling down and splitting of pairs are *not* compulsory, there are times when they are not advised. Just remember, you are forcing yourself to bet twice as much when you split a pair or double down. Therefore if the dealer has a good card up, approach with caution, not with habit. Here again "card counting" and knowing the remaining deck is a big help.

Card counting in the game of "21" may seem a little difficult to learn, but if you hope to succeed in the profession of gambling you certainly must take a businesslike or professional approach. If you don't want to work and just want to trust to luck, the casinos will love you, but you won't stay a winner for long. Suppose you are a "nonbeliever" and you are convinced everybody loses anyway, that is still no excuse for not putting forth an effort. Believe me, the player with an improved strategy losing just 1 percent will last ten times longer than the hunch player losing 10 percent overall. If you want to stay alive longer in blackjack, try learning my simple card counting method:

As each card is exposed, keep a running account up and down, for the high ones or the low ones. The "8" card is neutral, don't bother to count it when you see it. All below the 8 are small or low cards, all above the 8 (including aces) are large or high cards. For example, if you saw five cards, an ace, a 2, a 10, a 7, and a 9, that would be three high cards and two low cards. The score is now up one. Then, let's say you saw six more cards, a king, a 5, a jack, a 3, and two 6's. This would be two high cards and four low cards. It would take your running total down two from where it was, the score is now down one, or one below par.

Go through a deck for practice hundreds of times, dropping the cards singly, in pairs, in triples, and in bunches. Keep practicing up and down until you get fast at it. Use "cancellation"; let the neighboring high and low cards cancel each other and only count the remainders. Work out your own fastest way to count them, and see that when the deck is finished, you come out zero. Then you are ready to "count under fire." It takes time to count cards and not make mistakes, and meantime play your strategy. Then, in addition to that, you have money management to think about. Believe me, it takes practice, but it is most rewarding. Soon you will see what foolish bets other people will make.

Now, suppose you are a good card counter and it comes time to decide whether or not to split a pair or double down. On the doubling down or the pair splitting, if the remaining deck is mostly small cards, it is not a good idea. However, if you are pretty sure your chances are improved to get a big card, go ahead.

The fallacies of card counting are obvious also. When the deck is loaded with big cards, the dealer has an equal chance of getting a high score too, so don't raise your bet unless the remaining deck is plenty high, like a count of 4 or more out of the normal ratio. Also, the ideal time to raise your bet is when more than the normal ratio of aces is still remaining. The dealer wins if he gets the blackjack, and he will get it as often as you do; but if the chances of a blackjack are increased, you should raise your bet because if you hit it, you get 1½–1 odds. Therein lies your edge. Thus, card counting gives you a definite edge to know when to raise your bet and when to split pairs and when to double down.

Most casinos will shuffle the minute you make a big increase in your bet size, thus destroying the card counting edge. You have to "shop around" for a good place to play and be careful not to make your moves too obvious or too big.

The game of "21" is subject to too many changes to suit a career gambler. We beat the single decks for years. Then came a rash of changes. Now it is getting so single-deck dealers are hard to find. Nearly all the casinos on the Las Vegas Strip use the shoe or box for holding and dealing multiple decks.

Card counting still helps on multiple decks, but the opportunities take longer to materialize, and they must be magnified. For example, against a single deck, I would consider it favorable if there were four more big cards than little ones. Against a double deck, this has to be raised to 8; against a triple deck the count has to reach 12, etc. In favor of the multiple decks: Once the count does materialize, it usually lasts longer.

Many pages could be written on the foolish things players do in a "21" game. Following are a few very bad strategies: If you stand on less than 16 against a dealer good card up, your average loss on such a plan is worse than 20 percent! If you play using the same rules as the dealer, meaning going for a specific figure and ignoring all else, your loss is about 6 percent. You do not have that edge of going broke last or taking ties when you both go broke. The splitting of pairs can be very foolish and costly if not handled properly. Not a day goes by that a long-time player at a blackjack table doesn't see some nut come up and split 10's. To split 10's, 5's, or 4's is just asking to be licked. Not only are you giving away fair hands, you are paying twice as much for something unknown.

On the subject of automatically splitting aces, which is recommended by all authorities you read on the subject, I differ. The only time I will split aces is against a dealer poor card. Splitting aces costs you twice as much; you only get *one* card on each ace, and your chance of getting two big cards making them into two good hands is less than 25 percent. Your chances of drawing out to one good hand are much better. Remember, you have "soft" cards, and much manipulation is possible. L. G. H. says, "Don't split aces"; and if you play many thousands of hands of blackjack and keep track of results, some day you will come to agree with me and see that the other books are wrong on that point.

Another blanket recommendation of "21" authorities is to split 8's. This is OK most of the time, but I don't do it against a dealer 10. The splitting of 7's is only done against a dealer 4,5, or 6. The splitting of 2's, 3's, 6's, and 9's is usually a waste of time. Remember, splitting indifferent pairs forces you to start off with a poor count and to bet twice as much.

On the subject of doubling down, most players do it automatically on every 10 or 11. If you are not a counter or playing against a multiple deck, this is OK. Again I avoid spending twice as much when the likelihood of small cards is greatly increased. Become a good card counter and you will see the big difference. Hour after hour you will see people doubling down and splitting aces when you are almost sure they will catch little cards. They think they just had bad luck, but I prefer to deal in calculated risks and not trust to luck.

The rules of "21" differ in nearly every casino and area. Some do not offer an insurance bet; some allow double downs only on 10 or 11. The good old "soft" double down has all but disappeared. Unfortunately the game of "21" can be subject to increased changes and tightening and can cease to be a playable game for professionals.

A Good "21" Game

After much home practice and then under casino conditions for cheap chips, you should be ready for card counting and playing for real money. The L. G. H. winning procedure goes like this: Play the good normal strategy, taking it easy on splits and double downs; hold your action to a minimum unit bet as you count the cards and await a good run. When the deck gets "favorable," still do not raise the bet until you win two hands in a row or break into the right cycle pattern. It is foolish to bet big amounts in the teeth of a good dealer run.

It helps to keep the dealer from discovering you are a good card counter if you parlay your bets. To shove out a big bet all at once will invariably result in a shuffle. The L. G. H. strategy differs from other card counters who make a push every time the count turns favorable. You will find that favorable decks are just as favorable for the dealer, especially if he is already in a good run. Methods of wagering and debt recovery will be discussed further under Wagering and Cycle chapters.

BACCARAT

This is a fair game, increasing in popularity in American casinos. Nevada-style baccarat differs from chemin de fer in a few respects, mainly in that the house books all action. You can bet on either the player's or the banker's hand and have very close to an even-money chance. The bank has a wee edge. Consequently in the Nevada-type game the house charges 5 percent of your winnings if you bet on the bank and win. Since you might bet the bank about 50 percent of the time and win about 50 percent of those bets, this amounts to approximately 1.25 percent take for the house.

All baccarat payoffs are at even money. Of course you can get longer odds by parlaying or tripling your bet. There are no ties in baccarat; all tied hands are played over. The established rules are very strict; the player has no options on his hits and stands. In the European and older forms of this game, a good card counter could make more money. In a way, the simplicity of baccarat has its advantages; the player can concentrate on cycles and wagering plans.

The dealing box passes around the table to

each player in rotation, at which time he becomes the "banker," a mere formality. One player at a time at the table then becomes the "player." Other players at the table can bet on either hand at any time to make the best score. The perfect score is 9. All 10's and face cards in the deck are the same as 0, or as a 10. If you go past 9, a natural, you are still OK on the second ending figure of 9, as in 19. All casinos that play the game publish a rules card. Some charge a seat fee and most of them have a high minimum bet to keep the game expensive and exclusive. Here are the hit and stand rules.

PLAYER HAVING	BANKER HAVING	DRAWS WHEN GIVING	DOES NOT DRAW WHEN GIVING
1,2,3,4,5,10—Draws a card	3	1,2,3,4,5,6,7,8,10	8
6 or 7—Stands	4	2,3,4,5,6,7	1,8,9,10
8 or 9—Turns cards over	5	4,5,6,7	1,2,3,8,9,10
	6	6,7	1,2,3,4,5,8,9,10
	7	Stands	
	8 or 9	Turns cards over	

POKER, PAN, AND FARO

If you think you are a good poker player, try walking into the wolves' den and see if you still think so after a few days in Nevada. The house doesn't care who wins, as they get a seat fee or a small percentage of winning pots. What the tourist does not know is that expert poker players pay the house for the privilege of getting a crack at tourist money. My advice is to confine your card playing to private games with people you know and trust.

In games of pan and lo-ball, you have a similar situation; again, professionals are in there making a living off tourist money.

The game of faro has all but disappeared, and it doesn't look as if it will make a comeback. It takes a little too long to explain, and casinos haven't the time to educate new generations.

UPRIGHT WHEELS

These big old-time wheels of fortune are more or less for atmosphere and casual passers-by. They don't need a hidden brake such as you might find in carnivals; these wheels already have a tremendous percentage bite and are strictly for simple-minded suckers. All you have to do is count the spaces and check the odds offered; you will see that the percentage against you is 20 or more, no matter what kind of markings are on the wheel. Some have "Chuck-a-Luck" dice type of markings, some are all numbers. No matter if it is called Big Six, or any other name, pass the big wheel.

BINGO

This game should be confined to your church bazaar, where the profits would at least go to a good charity. The main purpose of bingo in Nevada is to keep bored wives occupied while the men play other games. You can get lucky at any game, but show me someone who beats it permanently, and I'll show you someone who either cheats or is house-sponsored. Shills in a bingo game hurt you more than shills in any other game, as they have playing cards too and can hit ahead of you.

KENO

The fabulous payoff prices make this a very popular casino game. It is like buying a sweepstakes ticket every fifteen minutes. You can get a lot of dreaming and wishful thinking for a small amount of money. The chances of winning $25,000 for one dollar are much worse than one in 25,000 but no one seems to care. Since millions of keno tickets are sold, there are bound to be lots of big winners. The ballyhoo and electric-lighted numbers all help to lure more dreamers. If you have money to spare, this is probably better than blowing it on sweets or drinks, so go ahead and enjoy yourself.

There are 80 numbers on a keno ticket; 20 are drawn for each game. The player marks small combinations or big combinations, from one number up to 11. You can play your favorite numbers, your age, birthday, special patterns, or any way you like. You can hook up numbers to be used as "key" figures in special multiple combinations. If you hit about half of the numbers you mark, you get a small payoff. There are enough little payoffs to continue tempting players into thinking they just could get lucky and hit a few more per ticket and collect the giant jackpots.

It is easy to get "hooked" on keno, but the professional gambler looks at the big percentage bite and decides to play a better game. For example, your chances of taking a dollar to the dice table and catching a prolonged good run are much better than your chances of hitting a giant keno payoff. It just takes longer. It is difficult to "recommend" any keno system, so please consider these as pastime suggestions. One way is to play your favorite combination continually, inexpensively, a little each day. Eventually you hit a fair return, and the little amounts you invested—even if they total a large amount—are forgotten.

Research into the game of keno points up many things. First, we find the worst bets are the longshots. Anyone playing the big string of numbers, 8 or more, in an effort to hit the $25,-000 maximum is taking the biggest beating in percentage. If you hope to hit the maximum jackpot, don't play 9 or 10 or more, stick to 8, which is bad enough.

The best spot on keno is a "two spot." Here the odds are 12½–1, when they should be 15–1, and that is the smallest "bite" in the game. All others are worse. The second best thing to play is a "one spot." Regarding which numbers to play, hold this in mind: Numbers that have been hitting in recent games are the hot ones, and they don't stay hot very long. When such a number cools off, it is just another number; so log the games and stick to small combinations of live numbers.

SLOT MACHINES

The only way to beat the slot machines is to own some. These "one-armed bandits" will not only grind you down, they will make you provide the muscle for the grinding wheels. Professional gamblers hate to see anybody hooked on fruit salad. The negative percentage varies from about 10 to as bad as 40. The tight ones are intermixed with the more liberal ones. The main appeal of slot machines is their simplicity; no thinking is required. If you know someone who claims he beats them, remember the example earlier in the book: it is possible this "lucky" person (if telling the truth) is still in the group that hasn't been ground down. Even the players who hit lots of jackpots are seldom aware of how much change they have spent.

ELECTRONIC GAMES

Electronic gambling devices also appeal to small bettors and passing tourists because they can play a game and not show their lack of knowledge or unwillingness to think. In most of the electronic games an added disadvantage is the limited number of coins they will accept, meaning a low table limit. Slot machines and electronic games are like pinball machines—strictly for cheap amusement.

DINNER SHOWS

The biggest bargains in Nevada and casino areas are the dinner shows. You pay no more for a good dinner than you would in any city restaurant, and get the best entertainers in the business thrown in as a bonus. It takes big names and good shows to bring in the people. The casinos spend fabulous amounts for their entertainment. You will gamble better and feel more like ladies and gentlemen of quality and leisure if you take time off to be entertained in high style. Advance reservations are advised for big name shows, and it helps if you check in at the casino-hotel complex that is playing the show you want to see. Some tourists are so awed by the magnificence of big hotel casinos that they check in at a nearby motel, not knowing that the casino rates are often just as reasonable.

HORSE RACING

Many times more professional speculators make a living on horse racing than on casino gaming. Race tracks are legal and handy to a hundred million people. Rising taxes and state and track percentages have hurt the profits of present-day race players, and the educational level of the public has risen, making it tougher on the professionals. Even so, it is still possible to find lots of good bets where percentage is actually in your favor.

The reason horse racing offers such an opportunity in spite of the big percentage "take" is the fact that the track only acts as a stakes holder for its percentage and the public sets the odds. Smart players concentrate on the places where the public sets a wrong price. Any "system" that wins at racing does so because it is proportionally underplayed. The sharp brains constantly seeking the profit spots keep shifting the values of winning systems. Many plans that worked years ago no longer do so today.

This is a world of fierce competition. It is evidenced in the racing industry itself where too many breeding farms are competing for the markets. There are thousands of thoroughbreds that never get to the races and, of those that do, thousands that never win a race. Racing has become big business with owners competing for millions in purses. Good old-fashioned trainers are scarce and the public trainers for hire are indifferent to the multitude of owners. New owners are burned out constantly, but more rush in with fortunes to fill the gaps. The overall result hurts the players, as horses are merely regarded as tools. If one isn't good enough, throw him away and get another.

Soundness in horseflesh is sacrificed for more speed and a victory by any means. This has a definite effect on handicappers and system players seeking reliability in their selections. Computer brains and careful handicappers are working against you; only the keenest of race players can earn a continued profit.

I am not just an "old timer" lamenting the "good old days." Each and every horse player is his own neighbor's enemy. You aren't trying to beat the tracks, you have to beat your fellow players. In the thirty years that I published speed and track variant advice and good systems and handicapping procedures, I helped cut my own profits. Now we must fight even harder to win.

As in casino games, it is appalling to see the naïve belief people will have in simple systems or their chances to win. In horse racing it is even more the case than on the gaming tables, for in horse racing it takes so long to prove or disprove a point. For example, 100 plays at a casino table can take only an hour or so to transpire, but some system on racing might not pick 100 plays in three months. Furthermore, 100 plays are a vastly inadequate basis for judging any plan. Consequently, race players jump to more false conclusions. They get sold on an idea much quicker and easier. Countless millions of race fans spend their entire lifetime changing systems and ideas, forever seeking a magic formula.

To win at racing nowadays you have to be guided by one main thought, "Do what the public does not do." This doesn't necessarily mean to go against the favorites, since a favorite is supposed to be the public choice. Every horse in the race has a certain percentage of public play, and the horses with the most obvious and logical good points will become the favorites. The trick is to do what the public does not do "proportionally." Even the most unlikely horse will have some crazy system pointing to him as a selection. Any horse in any race can be a proportional bargain in view of his percentage chance to win. For the most part, they are all victims of the big percentage bite, and bargains are hard to find.

Given some thirty rules to work with pertaining to various factors of handicapping, the system combination possibilities are virtually countless. To be constantly shifting rules and combinations seeking a system that wins is an endless research task. System sellers thrive on the curiosity of race fans. They spin a fairy tale about how they discovered this amazing winning formula and then offer to share it with you for a very nominal fee. Unfortunately, all sincere students of racing and gambling appreciate new or stimulating thoughts, so it is necessary for us to buy and read many things. Eventually, with a tremendous background of experience and ideas, through our own diligent research, we succeed in improving to the extent that we can show a little profit.

Because of the time projection and depth of understanding needed, race profits are tricky. One should really have a couple of years of records, numbering into hundreds or thousands of plays, before one could safely assume the method is reliable. Few people are willing to give racing this kind of study or effort.

To put together a winning plan on racing, it has to be reasonably logical so you are not dealing in extremely long-priced horses with proportionally longer gaps between winners. It is perfectly OK for your plan to point to favorites, or low-priced horses, so long as your percentage of winners, cross-multiplied by the prices you receive, will add up to a profit. What it amounts to is picking horses that are "overlays" in proportion to their chances.

It is a badly mistaken idea to assume that any horse going at longer odds than the morning line or some handicapper's line is automatically an "overlay." The line odds handicapper is but one man, subject to considerable human error and, more often, lacking ability to set the right price on each contender. On the subject of "overlays," a horse with a 50 percent chance could be an overlay at 6–5, whereas a horse with a 5 percent chance would be a bad buy at 10–1. It is not the odds, but the odds in view of his chances. This brings us back to a study of finding when the public is in error. It isn't a matter of their picking the wrong horse, for any selection method or approach will only get the winner a percentage of the time. The problem is purely one of price.

One way to approach getting a price edge is to utilize factors the public underestimates, or to pick a horse that violates some rule the public hates to go against. For example, the public hesitates to play a horse going up in class, or up in weight, or changing distance. While these factors may be a disadvantage to the horse, their disadvantage is not as great as the price indicates, hence a possible "overlay" appears.

Another way to improve your race earnings is to utilize factors the public does not incorporate into their calculations. Such a factor is "tote board betting action." A horse with what we call "live action" is one getting large sums of "non-public" money. This means the bettors of this added money must have a reason to believe the horse is better than it has shown in the visible past performances. Thus tote action becomes another dimension, or another factor in handicapping. It should be included in your calculations. The various ways to detect and use tote action will be given in the system chapter.

In addition to superior research, patience, and understanding, the successful race player has similar money management problems to those of the casino gambler. Besides money management and wagering there is the important psychological battle. The full racing picture will be completed when you put together the sections in this book on Wagering, Systems, and The Psychological Battle. It is up to you to put them together and use all your weapons if you hope to be a steady winner.

ESSENTIAL RESEARCH

Reading a book or instructions on "how to do" something does not qualify you as an expert. Ability increases with practice and work. In race playing and casino gambling there is no substitute for work, experience, and personal research. More than 90 percent of all horse players and casino visitors go into the game with inadequate study and research behind them. Some have a very mistaken idea of what spending time on a subject means. Their approaches are more often casual, sporadic, and very unscientific. They accept all sorts of opinions and comments without verifying them.

Back in the 1940's, I had been working at my profession full time for about ten years. I was talking to an attorney who was a success in his profession. In our discussion of various factors on racing, he stopped me, saying in effect, "Young man, I have been studying racing for thirty-five years. What makes you think you know more about it than I do?"

I asked him if he had practiced law steadily since he got out of school, and got an affirmative answer. He added that he had put his kids through college.

Finally, I asked, "And have you led a normal family life, with other activities besides racing?"

He said he had.

"OK," I said. "Now if you have been busy in your profession and other things, how many hours a day have you spent in race research?" He got my point. Then I told him that for over ten years I had studied racing about fourteen hours a day. In terms of hours of serious work, then, I had probably studied it ten times as much as he had.

My attorney friend asked me, "Do you really have to work at it that hard in order to beat it?"

Once more I answered his question with a question, "Were you an instant success, or did it take a lot of work to get to the top in your profession?"

The whole problem with most players is that they want success without work. Their mental picture of a successful gambler is like the Hollywood image—some guy betting big money and doing nothing but win. Well, gambling is a *profession* that takes hard work to learn and skill to stay on top. You can't buy an education and say, "Stick it in my head." You can't become an athlete sitting in your easy chair and watching sports events on television. It isn't until you turn away from the dream world and get down to real work that you get on the right track.

Do you think the medical schools hand a student doctor surgical instruments after he has read about an operation, and say, "Now, you do it"? No indeed! He has to practice a lot on cadavers and dummies, and he has to start at the bottom and build his knowledge and skill.

In gambling or race playing, you need a background of well-implanted knowledge and facts; then you need plenty of preliminary practice and study. Most of all, you need the tools of the trade to work with. No horseplayer worth his salt has fewer than a year's back Racing Forms or Telegraphs on hand for checking purposes.

The prospective casino gambler should accumulate thousands of recorded transactions, and *actual* ones acquired cheaply under fire. Only then will the gambler acquire the depth of understanding needed for successfully working at his trade. It doesn't matter if you use toy roulette wheels and throw your own dice at home, do it for not hundreds but thousands of decisions. Don't dash to the nearest betting place the minute something looks good. Go further and get the real facts.

CYCLES AND PATTERNS

One day at a dice table, I was hitting them pretty good, often moving my chips from the front to back line and vice versa. The fellow next to me was losing. He said to me, "You are guessing them pretty good."

I shook him up a bit with my answer, "What makes you think I'm guessing?"

He quickly regained his composure and voiced a typical opinion, "It's all a matter of who is lucky."

To this I said, "You can use luck or ESP or whatever you want. Personally, I think *any* system is better than no system at all."

As a matter of fact, I have, in recent years, tried to make my casino play appear as casual and "just lucky" as possible. I don't want to attract attention. Even so, I have had players study my action intently, and I have had them try to get me to tell them a formula for when to make certain bets. They have seen me play, forging ahead little by little, while other players come and go. Occasionally, I have a spectacular winning run, but usually so do the other players at the table at that time, so my win is not the only one. However, not infrequently, when the winning run comes on the back line, the winning players (including me) are few in number.

One night I was playing back line in a good run. It had gone seven or eight, and winnings were getting bigger. A fellow next to me was doing the same thing. Suddenly he said, "The *don't* can't win much more." And he switched his bets to the *pass line*. So help me, he went broke in the next six rolls, while the back line kept on winning and I made an even bigger pile. That is lesson number one you learn from research of cycles and patterns, "Don't buck a run." If you don't like it, lay off, but don't figure on its turning *until* it does.

People constantly go broke in casinos believing a thing can't get any worse. Some think that in order to break a bad run you should change tables. Sometimes this seems to work, but the thing might have changed the very next hand after they walked away. And they just could walk into another bad run at the new table, actually producing a longer one than if they had stayed at the first table.

Cycle and pattern study teaches us that *one* winner is good for terminating or breaking a slump, but it doesn't necessarily mean the start of a winning streak. It takes more than one to convince me the tide has turned. Many players think it is a good system to follow the last winner or last two, as it should get them in on all winning streaks in that direction. True, but they will get clobbered by the "chops" or "zigzags" which are sufficiently interspersed to destroy their profits.

In an even-money game, a good run isn't two or three, nor is that even a good time to start in that direction or against it. Many players figure that after three or four on a side, it is now time to play the other side because of the law of averages. According to their reasoning, you can't lose if you eliminate that many losers. What they fail to consider is that all big slumps must have a small beginning and all too frequently they are walking right into the record breakers. There are arguments on both sides, and only research will settle the matter. Check fifty thousand plays and you will know the answers.

In my personal research I have checked over a million actual tabulations of the games. Dice runs are personally acquired, and I have logged beyond six figures on roulette. Voluminous European roulette records have been printed, which I have also studied. You might also be interested in knowing that lengthy tabulations have been fed into giant computer brains. These studies *have cracked* pattern and cycle and have demonstrated that a profit can be made on supposedly unbeatable games. The impossible of yesterday is routine today.

Here is your key to pattern: There are five basic types of runs. Short and long runs on either side, and erratic. The solution is really very simple. When the plays are running in bunches, play them to continue bunching. When they are erratic, either stop or play them to continue erratic. Anyone who can see only the straight runs has very limited thinking.

For one thing, I'm convinced the main fault in the thinking of the professors and mathematicians is that they are bound to laws and theories based on random numbers. Dice, roulette, games, and cards do not run in the same cycles as computerized random numbers. The cycles in each game are different even though they all have similar odds plays and percentage bites.

What we are trying to do is capitalize on the fact that winners and losers come in bunches. The longer the odds, the more this bunching is obvious. Suppose you take an individual number on a roulette wheel. Let's say you picked number 17 on the American game. There are 36 numbers and two green slots (0 and 00), or 38 possibilities. Do you think the 17 would go 37 misses and then hit, go 37 misses and hit, then go 37 more and hit? This exact pattern might not happen in a million spins. What would happen is that some 17's would be close together, and then there would be gaps of great length. If you will remember our statement that *one* winner does not necessarily herald a winning streak, you are on the right track. An individual number is good when it gets "warmed up" a bit, and pretty bad when it is "cold." In the system section I will explain how to benefit from hot numbers.

Examples of wrong thinking pop up all the time in a casino. If two long shots come in together (repeaters), most people and even the dealers will say it can't hit three. Some will even quote a figure like "one in 5,000 possibility." Well, the one in 5,000 would be close *before* the streak started, but once it hit, that figure no longer applies. And if it hit twice, it is still a normal chance on the third hit.

Mathematicians will say a roulette number always has one chance in 38 (American wheel) or a dice longshot like 12 is always a 35–1 shot. Here is where L. G. H. and the mathematicians part company. I say the longshots get a whisker better when they are "warmed up" or "bunching." I can't say *why*. Call it the "law of attractions," or whatever you like, but my research indicates this attraction works. Now, and this is an important point: Some of the longshots have too much negative percentage against them for this cycle improvement to overcome. This is the case at some of the dice odds offered, but not so on roulette. If you like longshots on any game, my advice is to play them only when they are hot. It helps a little. If these hints on cycles haven't kindled your interest in further investigation, then you can stay in the group with the lazy ones and nonbelievers.

The fact that research *is* work, and even good methods can have tremendous slumps, creates a lot of nonbelievers. Take a longshot method, like individual roulette numbers (35–1 shots); you don't need hundreds of units capital, you need *thousands*. You don't get your profit every hour; sometimes it takes days!

You can't judge racing by a day at the races and you can't judge a dealer or a table by half a dozen hands. If you are interested in successful systematic speculation, part of the learning process is lengthy research on cycles and patterns. After a while doors will open and you will see things in an entirely different light.

In roulette, using a pencil and paper is acceptable. In Europe it is a very common practice. Just why Americans have no respect for system players I do not know. You will find much better players on the Continent and, I might add, a lot more winners. For my roulette game I use little folded-down cards. I prefer to be inconspicuous. Since system players are kidded or asked questions, I prefer to cut down on the distractions as much as possible.

On dice you do not need a pencil and paper, as you have a regular abacus right in front of you. The way you place your different denomination chips in the grooved rack can tell you many things. Other players don't even pay attention or understand your way of stacking chips. For example, if you had two denominations of chips, $5 chips and $1 chips, you could stack them alternately indicating passes and misses. If you only had one denomination of chips, slant some toward you to indicate passes, slant some away to indicate misses. A glance down will quickly tell you what has transpired. Your playing chips come from a different pile. Some chips have ring marks on the edges. These too can tell a story when you look down at them.

In a rack just one section long (less than one foot), I keep track of passes, misses, field runs, 6 and 8 runs, and my debt standing. I know exactly what I am doing at all times. When you cut down to a simpler system and do not intermix plays, it is no problem to keep this information in your head. All it takes is a little practice.

WAGERING PLANS

Up to this point I have tried to show you the difference between good bets and bad. No wagering plan on Earth can continually overcome a gigantic negative percentage. Clever and intelligent wagering *can* turn a small loss into a profit but, if you continue to make bad percentage bets, no one can help you. Assuming, then, that you will stick to the right plays, you are ready for this important part.

Perhaps you have a wrong impression of what it means to "beat the races" or to "beat the casinos." If you expect to take a few hundred dollars and make a living or a thousand or two every month, you are on the wrong footing. If you think you can take a five- or a ten-dollar bill into a gaming casino and walk out with your pockets full, you are a dreamer. Of course those things have happened, but they are very rare.

In a normal business, a small percentage profit on the capital invested is considered a good return. On money at interest, 10 percent is a high rate. The professional race player and gambler can operate on a small percentage profit because his rate of "turnover" is very swift. The dice can be thrown up to two hundred times an hour. A roulette wheel can make up to one hundred decisions an hour. (The dice wouldn't be making two hundred passes or misses per hour, just throws. However, it is possible to get fifty or sixty decisions an hour.) Anyway you look at it, you get fast turnover. You don't have to make big bets or a big profit every transaction; you can afford to take it slow and careful.

If the "burned out" race player or gambler who has tried many, many times through the years would look back, I think he would find the main cause was "miscalculation" and inadequate planning. He makes many "false starts" and then has to back off and try a different course. Each false start or miscalculation that is *not recovered* adds to the loss pile, which grows too large a burden for a new plan to pick up. This is part of the cost of learning, but many such losing ventures could have been avoided if the player had only taken the time to think or research a thing through. Let's start our wagering plan thinking at the bottom and then build it step by step.

"Flat play" in wagering means always betting the same amount. The only place flat play has a chance is on excellent handicapping and spot plays in horse racing. If you always play the same amount on a casino bet and give away a little percentage, you will find it really mounts up fast. Winning or losing percentage will *compound* itself. You can lose $100 a day on flat play just betting small amounts. So let's forget the flat play. On the other hand, you can lose a fortune quickly if you progress too steeply, and just hit one really bad slump that exceeds table limits or your capital limits.

"Living on borrowed time" applies to most steep progressions and foolish wagering plans. To start with a simple example, players quickly learn the stupidity of "doubling up to get even": 1,2,4,8,16,32,64,128,256,512—in nine times you are up to where you must bet over 1,000 to get even and only make *one* unit profit. Believe it or not, hardly a day goes by at any gambling table that does not see players try this. Such players figure they will progress a "few times" and walk away with a profit. Some do get away with it, but it seemed so easy, soon they try it again. Just a question of time——

The next step tried by gamblers is to slow down the rate of climb. This may be done by single units, like 1,2,3,4,5,6,7,etc., or by series, like 1,1,1,2,2,2,3,3,3,4,4,4,etc. This is an improvement in borrowing more time, but its faults soon become evident. It borrows more time, but meantime it makes less money. After a prolonged slump, the increasing rate is insufficient to overcome the negative percentage. When you increase from 1 unit to 2 units, that is a 100 percent increase, but when you go from 30 to 31, that's only 3 percent.

The third step in the thought process of a gambler playing with figures is to try to cure the ills of step two. Now he tries a "rise-and-fall" application on the scales. When you lose you go up a notch, when you win you drop back. This seems to work a little better for a little longer. Some short-term gamblers like it very much. I say "short-term" gamblers, because this one too has faults if you go on long enough. It finally works its way up to where it is zigzagging and climbing and along comes a "slump on top of a slump" when the losses mount swiftly. One bet now equals all the hard-earned profits of hours before. The player may run out of nerve, out of money, or out of time long before the selections hit a good winning streak. Or, as mentioned in the paragraph above, the power of the rate of increase may now be less than the negative percent it is asked to overcome.

Another direction the wagering plan student takes in his study of plans is to try the "due column" approach, or dividing the debt by the odds. Actually, this is no different from "doubling up." On "doubling up," the odds are calculated to work on "even money," calling for 100 percent increase each time. What difference does it make if the odds are 3–1 and you bet one-third of the debt instead of the full debt? Your climb is slower, but your winners are proportionally less frequent—same end result: the climb gets too steep, gets out of reach.

A still different wagering plan that crops up every day in a busy casino is the "cancellation." There are many variations of this famous oldie, and it is amazing that people discovering it for the first time think they have really found the pot of gold. It seems to work a little bit longer than previously mentioned ones, but again basically it is the same principle. The reason the cancellation lasts longer than the doubling up is that it doesn't try to get out of the hole all on *one* winner. The cancellation will survive at even-money odds if you can get better than one-third winners. This, it would seem, is a cinch to do on even-money bets, dice, "21," or roulette.

To play the cancellation (which I am not recommending, only explaining), you need a pencil and pad. You start by writing down a short string of figures, like 1,2,3,4. Now you are ready to start betting. Your next bet is always the sum of the two figures on the opposite ends of the string. In the above example, it is $1 + 4$, or 5. So you bet the 5. If it wins, you strike off the 1 and 4, thus: $\cancel{1}$,2,3,$\cancel{4}$. Now, you only have remaining in the string the figures 2 and 3. Again the next bet is 5, since $2 + 3 = 5$. If this one wins, you have cleaned up your string with a profit, and you can quit, or you can start a new string.

Now, let's see how it goes when you do not win them all. Start again with 1,2,3,4, the bet is 5. Let's say the 5 loses, the string now reads 1,2,3,4,5, and the new bet is the sum of the two ends, 1 + 5 or 6. Let's say the 6 wins, you strike off the 1 and 5, thus: 1̸,2,3,4,5̸, and the next bet is the sum of the ends, 2 + 4, or 6. This time let's say the 6 loses, you have to enter it on the end of the string. Your bet guide now reads: 1̸,2,3,4,5̸,6. Since the figure 1 is dead, the two uncanceled ends are 2 and 6, the next bet is 8. Continue to repeat the process, adding to the end the last amount you bet if you lost it, knocking off the two ends when you win one. This works great, you may say. So it does, "on borrowed time," but the time comes when it gets pretty steep.

If you like the way this plan looks, try it on paper and see how much capital it takes in the prolonged worst stretches of even-money plays you can find. For the man with plenty of capital and intestinal fortitude, this plan isn't too bad.

You might go a few days or a week thinking you had Nevada licked before you found *with cash* how bad the "cancellation" can get at its worst. Don't take my word for anything. Unfortunately the only knowledge that sticks is the hard-earned kind.

Earlier I said the gambler doesn't need a large percentage of profit because the action is pretty fast, he gets lots of "turnover." Why not try a more "safe and sane" scale of gradual increase? This gradual rise should remain constant and not lose its potency as a fixed-unit one would do when it got a long way from base. "Back to base" in wagering terminology means the starting point. When a plan gets back to base, it should be out of the hole with a profit. Then you start over.

"Fixed percent scales" are pretty good, and they can be used in various ways. They can be used as "no retreat" increases, or "rise and fall." On the "no retreat," you advance after each loser, by a fixed percentage increase over your last bet. You continue to bet the larger amount until you win out. A 10 percent increase scale is quite adequate for careful players (10 percent will not be enough if you insist on bucking bad games where your flat play loss exceeds 10 percent—remember no plan can save bad selections). To play the fixed percent scales on a rise-and-fall basis, you have to note the "bet number" rather than the amount. On gradual scales the amount does not always increase in an obvious manner. You might be playing 1 unit 5 times before you go to 2. Thus, if you were on the fourth bet and won it, you would go back to the third and, in both cases, you would still be betting only *one unit.*

You may be thinking: What's the point in that? How can it make any money or recover losers if it isn't increased? Permit me to recommend your best friend—Mr. Research. He will help bring home many points such as, Remember, you have *time,* take it slow and easy and you won't get burned. The beauty of a plan that is betting 1 or 2 shows up when you hit a nasty downbeat. Then when you are up to betting 3 or 4 and the winners start coming, you make a nice quick recovery. A very important friend is Mr. Research. If you get to know Research well, you will learn how to win and have the understanding that sees the folly in what so many foolish players are doing.

Wagering improvements can be accomplished in several ways: (1) leveling off, (2) stop-loss, (3) delayed climb, and (4) slump-breaking.

On the scale plan just illustrated, more conservative players can "level off" at a given level, such as 5 units or 10 units. Stay at this level until a recovery is accomplished.

A stop-loss can prevent a tremendous loss in a superslump, the record-breaking kind, when to go on past a certain point costs tremendously. This stop-loss should be set quite high because,

	BET NUMBER	UNIT AMOUNT

On the scale on the right we show two columns, Number and Amount→

The player keeps track of the bet number, then matches it up with the indicated amount. The amount is in units. These units can be any figure: 25¢ per unit, $1 per unit, $2, $5, $10, etc.

The play is started by wagering bet number 1, which calls for 1 unit. If this loses, the next bet is bet number 2, which also calls for an amount of 1.

The player need not keep track of profit and loss if he uses a rise-and-fall plan, for whenever he gets back to base there will be a profit.

If the player wants to use the scale on a no retreat basis, then he must keep track of the balance since last time at base. As soon as there is a profit, return to base, bet number 1.

To use this scale on a rise-and-fall basis, the bet advances or rises one number after a loser. Example: if the fifth bet at 1 unit lost, next bet (the sixth) calls for 2 units bet. If number 6 wins, go back one bet number and play the fifth, 1 unit.

Note, it is wise to keep track of losses since last time at base even when playing the rise-and-fall way; you can return to base any time you are ahead, even if your indicator isn't back to bet number 1. The closer and the longer you stay near base, the safer the plan.

The scale can also be used on price ranges other than even money. Go up one bet number after each loser, but come down in bet numbers as many points as the odds-to-one. Example, if on the eleventh bet, playing 3 units and you won a 2–1 bet, your next bet number would be number 9.

Try this scale through your research and you will see that it weathers much tougher stretches than other plans and yet comes out with a profit and not too much capital involved.

Capital recommendations: The greater the reserve the better. Should have 500 units reserve to play on a 1-unit basis. A 1000 reserve would be better and should suffice through any good kind of selections where the percentage against the player is small. (Dice lines, single-0 roulette, expert "21.")

BET NUMBER	UNIT AMOUNT
1	1
2	1
3	1
4	1
5	1
6	2
7	2
8	2
9	2
10	3
11	3
12	3
13	4
14	4
15	5
16	5
17	6
18	7
19	8
20	9
21	10
22	11
23	12
24	14
25	16
26	18
27	20
28	22
29	25
30	28
31	30
32	32
33	35
34	40
35	45
36	50
37	55
38	60
39	70
40	80
41	90
42	100
43	110
44	120
45	135
46	150

once you accept one, it takes a long time to earn it back. A low point stop-loss is worthless, as most plans will hit it often enough to wipe out the hard-earned gains. Mr. Research can help you here.

The delayed climb is one of your best weapons. Instead of increasing your bet units or number after each loser, hold the bet the same until a winner comes, then pick up the climb or plan where you left off. This takes further advantage of good runs as well as holds losses down in bad ones. Paperwork and checking are highly advised.

Slump-breaking is similar to stop-loss and delayed climb. Action is stopped after the losers pass a given point, then resumed when the winners start coming in again. In all of these attempts at improving the situation one frequently meets with frustration; the very next play after you stopped may be a needed winner. In time you will get to where the frustrations do not bother you, they are part of the game. If you are following definite rules, you must know from research that the new pattern of winners and losers that you are creating *is* an improvement even though it also has its rough spots.

I have outlined various basic wagering concepts. The interested and determined student will accept the challenge and spend many hours working with figures. You should come up with ideas of your own and adaptations of wagering ideas.

Do not commit the common error of making the wagering plan fit *known* results. After you have what appears to be *the* plan that suits you, try it over a prolonged different and new set of results. The more paperwork and home practice you do, and the more cheap chip testing you do, the less likely you are to encounter big losses and bitter disappointment at the "living wage" level. Gambling can be fun and a great satisfaction when you win.

CAPITALIZATION

Most players badly underestimate the tremendous capital reserve needed for survival in gambling or race playing. This is partly due to insufficient research and experience, but it is also due to their mental inability to grasp the tremendous scope and magnitude of the swings of the game. In horse racing, due to the time element between races and between days, a person can be kidding himself a lot longer timewise than in casino gambling. Because of the shorter string of results researched, proportionally more horseplayers miscalculate their capital requirements.

The average race system offered on the market gives a page of past results—a mere snap of the fingers in terms of time. Any race system that hasn't been checked for hundreds of plays cannot be trusted.

On casino action, judge only by thousands. I have voluminous records at my disposal and have easily checked over half a million gaming transactions. I have averaged a few hours a day in research for more years than the age of many who will read this book. Even so, with all my study and experience, I still encounter "crazy swings" that break a record for how bad or how good something can go.

Gambling casinos, with thousands of transactions of all different kinds, going for the house all day long, have still been known to encounter periods when the house has a serious run on the bank, and periods of days on end when the house runs in the red. Imagine, then, if they have percentage in their favor and it can get that bad, how bad can it get for *you* with percentage against you! Casino owners and managers can get into some real sweats in a downbeat. In fact, many go broke and have to seek new bankrolls. There can be prolonged periods when a table will do nothing but lose. The changing of dealers, decks, or dice will not stop the run. Old Man Percentage doesn't swing back until he is good and ready. How far can it go? Frankly, I don't know. I haven't lived long enough. Let us consider the capital required for each game.

Do you know what the house considers an adequate bankroll for a "21" table? Shouldn't your bankroll be the same? I wonder how many players going into the game have $5,000 or so. I have seen the house bring over $5,000 at a time in big chips and keep them coming. Now that I have sobered you adequately, let's get down to the common man's level. First, assuming you are playing a good strategy and *not* giving away any percentage, then you *might* survive on flat play with 300 units. If you are using any sort of a progression, you should have more.

On roulette there are all kinds of odds brackets and all kinds of ways to play. The longer the odds, the greater the swing potential and the more capital you should hold in reserve. Once, starting with 25¢ chips and playing my 35-1-shot game, I built my gains up to $1,800 over a period of about two months. I gave it all back in one night after I moved up to the $1 level on a mild progression. Of course, that effected an "improvement" in my rules and my capital hasn't run out since, *but it can,* as records are forever being broken.

My advice is to avoid double-0 roulette wheels. On single-0 wheels, the capital required varies according to the game you play. About 2,000 units are suggested for long-shot approaches or 500 units for shorter odds. This is flat play; progression takes more. My favorite roulette game—all three even-money propositions at once—is capitalized at 1,500 units, or three banks of 500 each. Your units can be any size, depending on the table or area you play.

An important point in capitalization is this: You don't necessarily need a lot of money, but you *do* need to play chip size in proportion to your reserve. About 95 percent of all players underestimate the capital requirements. Those playing for $5 chips should be playing for $1, and those playing for $1 should be playing for 25¢.

I have often been at a table, with hundreds in reserve in my pocket, playing on a conservative scale, and along comes some "big shot" shooting for bigger chips. He sneers at small-chip players. But pretty soon he gets a little red-faced after dropping a bundle and leaves the table. I bet the big chips, too, but not with *my money*. My big-chip betting is done on *their money* in a prolonged good run. At that time I don't have to be holding five hundred times my bet in reserve!

On dice, one of the most popular approaches, played by most of the High Rollers, is to bet the *pass line,* then take odds on the point if one comes out. Following that, they play "come" and take odds. Some can't wait for the "come" and free odds, they have to buy the *place* numbers. In any case, they are playing a game of 7's. Sevens can come up quite a few in a row, or they can go a few dozen times with none showing. The High Roller's game can swing violently in either direction. Generally, of course, it varies up and down in a routine way, with a gradual—almost painless—downward sink. Those buying *place* numbers sink a little faster. The good High Roller is alerted for a good upswing, tries to push his action and make a killing. The really good player does his best to hang on and quit well ahead.

Now, how much capital should one have to play such a game? I will bet you that not one in a thousand of those playing it even know. Money to them comes from their business or profession —some source other than gambling. If they lose, so what! They will go home, come back again some other day, and try again. Once in a while they make a nice win.

I have researched their game and envy them not. Their betting is too unorganized and un-controllable. They are purely playing the swings. OK, how far can it swing? My research indicates they should have 1,000 units of capital for a game of 7's. Mr. Big, if you are playing table limits, are you holding one thousand times that in reserve? On a $500 table, that means half a million dollars! Fortunes can be made in gambling. But you sure had better know your business, because fortunes can also be lost in gambling.

For the good dice game of playing the *lines* (skipping the *place* numbers and all the other propositions on the table) one should approach with a few reserve banks of at least 200 units each. I call these "sub-banks." I drop a subbank once in a while, but I make it back before I drop all my sub-banks, or total bankroll.

Now let's consider the capital needed in race playing. This depends on whether or not you are playing it for fun or going to the track every day and trying to make a living wage. Very few people are realistic about the game, or have even given it adequate thought. Transportation, track admission, parking, race forms, programs, eating, etc., amount to about $10 a day. Add another $20 a day for the cost of living, and to make a wage at racing one should earn at least $30 a day.

To make $30 a day on the races, a good player would have to bet an average of at least $120, assuming he can earn 25 percent profit on the dollar. If he earns 10 percent, he'll have to bet an average of $300 a day. Now, if he plays carefully and not foolishly, let's say he makes three bets a day. This means he is forced to play between $40 and $100 per bet. Thus we arrive at the bet amount needed. The reserve should be many, many times the bet amount. You are not really ready to make a living at race playing with less than $2,000. You should have $10,000. Does that make your present job look better? Are you sure you want to be a professional gambler? Remember it takes *work* to earn that elusive flat play profit on which the above figures are based. If you are going to play a progression on a losing game, Heaven help you.

A good rule by which to judge a system is to research it until it has earned two or three times what you consider an adequate playing bankroll. If you set your bankroll to play it at 100 units, then see that it has earned a few times that over a period of hundreds of plays or more. Considering how few actual months of play and how small a number of plays a race method gets in a month, the average player has no concept at all of how well or poorly his plan can swing. Again this is why so many systems that look good are really illusions, for they were viewed in only a small part of an upswing.

A crude, but somewhat effective, way to judge the potential swing of a system is to multiply by twenty the size of the maximum payoff odds it gets. Favorites, for example, pay up to 3–1, can downswing 60 units. This, of course, is assuming you are using "further selected" favorites. You can't just play all favorites, as that is a losing game and can keep on going down.

When you consider how much capital one needs to go into a small business nowadays, racing or gambling stacks up favorably. Investigate how much a franchise costs for a little business such as an ice cream store or a hamburger drive-in. Investigate how much it would cost you to open any kind of store or office. You'll find it runs into thousands before you are ready to open your doors. Then what makes you think you can take a few hundred and jump into making big money at racing or gambling? Be a little more realistic and fair to the game! Make sure your capitalization is adequate.

A strong point of capitalization is to use subbanks and a stop-loss on each. Since we never know how far a downswing can go, it helps to set a limit. Remember the important rule: Limit your losses, but don't limit your gains. If you are a bit weak on will power or get carried away with gambling fever, don't take your entire bankroll with you. I consider that it is very bad policy to have credit or check-cashing ability at a casino.

All too often a gambler gets the urge to "shoot the works." In World War II they had an expression, "Go for Broke." All I can say is, if you "Go for Broke," broke you will surely go. If you try it once with a 50–50 chance and succeed, you will invariably try it again. Those who will try it twice will try it three times, and so on. Their chance of survival is very minute.

It is pretty hard to build up to an adequate playing bankroll so, once you have it, don't get foolish and throw it away in a few minutes of wild play. The name of the game is "money." Enjoyment from the game depends on the individual. If his money comes easily from some other business, he may get his kicks out of blowing it. The true full-time gambler enjoys increasing his bankroll and beating a tough opponent to do it.

SYSTEMS

Are there such things as winning systems? Definitely yes. Then why aren't there more winning-system players? There are many, many reasons. They fall by the wayside because of miscalculating the capital, patience, or work involved. Too many players don't want a system; they want a miracle. Their idea of a system is some magic formula that does nothing but fill their pockets with money. Nothing less is considered any good. The professional speculator is darned glad to have a plan that wins, period.

Many systems look good on paper, where time and decisions under pressure are not a factor. Under actual playing conditions the plan may be too wild or too tough to follow. A player not only has to pick a good system that stands up under research but one that fits his needs and personality. In listing methods that have been satisfactory for me, I must advise the reader that no plan carries a guarantee. Only your own current lengthy research is to be trusted. Some plans that worked on horse racing years ago are no longer profitable.

The weekend or short-term gambler and infrequent race track visitor may find good systems too conservative. Shortness of time and impatience are no excuse for playing every race or making bad percentage bets. It is very easy to dabble away hard-earned profits while waiting for the good plays to come along. The system goes on showing a profit long after the player has gone broke or dropped it.

An expert player can handle more than one thing at a time. This is fairly easy in playing the races, but can get complicated in casino action. One might think that the more plans he has in action, the more stability it gives the play. This isn't always true. Your demise can be hastened sometimes if all your good plans hit a slump at the same time and you were playing them all out of one capital pool. The game is full of little traps, and it takes experience and vision to keep from getting caught.

Many a famous race player or gambler has been known to scoff at systems but, to a man, they all have been very systematized. They just didn't realize that their testing of luck and pushing the runs was all pretty much by rules. Actually everything we do is by system, so let's stop looking down on the word and get to work.

Racing Systems

As horse racing becomes more competitive and more and more sharp brains and computers work harder to extract profits, the player's task gets tougher and more complicated. Old-fashioned "extremely tight and logical" systems just won't pay any more. Of course, any coincidental combination of rules can hit hot streaks and give a race player a temporary charge. The really serious students know that the method has to go on for a longer time.

The first method I like is quite illogical to dyed-in-the-wool handicappers and system players. This one calls for a play on a *first starter*. This is a horse with no racing record at all—no established speed or class, no consistency, no known reliability to attract the rules player. Ah, but the secret to success is the fact that we only play *certain* first starters, not *all* first starters. The ones we like have "tote action." Here is where the power comes in. Here is an unknown horse, and yet he is backed by heavy money. In a race containing just average horses you frequently find a superior horse that is totally unknown. No investor in his right mind will dump thousands on an ordinary horse making his first start. He waits until the horse has experience and has proved his ability.

So where did the heavy action come from on the first starter we propose to play? It had to come from the connections who know the horse's superior ability. The rule to catch such plays?

Very simple. If a first starter goes off *favorite*, it is a play. If he goes second choice, but has had virtually no mention and is a tremendous underlay from estimated odds, this, too, is a play.

Further on the subject of profitable first starters, when only one goes at long odds in a race with poor-quality maidens, he, too, is worth a try. He may not be any good, but at least he hasn't proved himself yet to be bad. On this latter type you need long odds.

Now don't go overboard on first starters, and also don't jump to conclusions after checking a small number of these plays. Be businesslike and judge by a large number of plays. There is a nice profit there for cautious and smart speculators.

To refine further the approach mentioned in the racing chapter, you can put together a profitable system based on a horse that violates commonly used public rules. I call this horse a "multiple switcher." Look for a horse changing class (preferably going up), changing distance, going up in weight, changing track conditions, changing jockey. The more of these changes the better. There must be at least three. This, too, can put you onto some longshots; so, remember, longshots have longer slumps and therefore take more capitalization.

A real longshot type of horse to play is what I call a "maximum class climber." This horse is improving steadily and keeps climbing and surprising people by winning every now and then at terrific odds. To find these, we look at the bottom race in each horse's visible past performances. The play is the one who, way back, several races ago, ran for the cheapest level of any in the race. Today the horse must be within fifteen days of his last outing.

On the subject of class maneuvers to find a system play, this one seems pretty good, even though it is well known. The reason it pays is the fact that the horse's last race may have been a bad one. The public goes mostly on what a horse did on his very last outing. This "up and down class" play must have won his second race back, by two or more lengths, going away in the stretch. Then, he stepped up in class and lost his last race. Today he steps back down a bit. His winning race had to be within the last twenty-one days.

A little profit can still be made in racing by expert speed and class handicapping in the traditional style. The key here is to do a much better job than the public. The use of pace figures and track variants is a little beyond the average player, so any serious handicappers who go to all that added trouble are usually rewarded. To the persons preferring to follow race tracks, my recommendation is to do good work and also to pick the smaller tracks. Lots of good old systems still work at the minor tracks that no longer work at the majors. A fine old system is to take "stand-out favorites" to place and use "tightener" rules to eliminate the unprofitable ones. Tightener rules mean: good recent race, top speed, good jockey.

Many race players specialize successfully in certain types of horses. Some go for a lazy long-shot approach that does fairly well. All you have to do is read the Racing Form list of "horses in trouble." Then check the alphabetical listing to see which are going today. It helps if you keep a little notebook and date the horses. Play those coming back from an "in trouble" race if they do so within two weeks. Persons more than casu-ally interested in racing will read all result charts and will also keep a list of horses with "bad signs." Avoid any the chart caller says pulled up sore and avoid those with comments like "bore out" or "weakened." This cuts many losers off any method you are following.

A good specialization is to concentrate on horses claimed on either their last race or the second race back. If the claim was within twenty-one days, the horse makes a good pros-pect in today's race. Horsemen live by the cleverness of their claims. Confine your action to four- and five-year-olds. Additional handicapping-tightening rules can be used if you like.

Shortcut handicapping is usually of no value because simple factors are also seen and used by the general public. My favorite shortcut is a strange one that the public seems to ignore. I call it "handicapping by odds." If a horse shows any good factors, down go the odds. If a horse has tote action, down go the odds. Better jockey, lower odds, and so forth. The trick is to get a horse that went down sharply last out and missed, counting on the horse making amends today.

The system rule goes like this: If the horse cut to less than half in odds last out, play him today. For example, if he was 10–1 two races back, and 4–1 on his last race, something caused the big drop, so we figure he is an improving horse. If the reader will tabulate scores or hundreds of plays by any good system rules, he can then find a wagering plan that fits the situation. One should compile lengthy summaries on any system before rushing out to play it. No matter how it looks, allow much more capital than seems necessary.

A reverse of the system in the preceding paragraph also seems to work. Look for a horse who was short odds at least two out of his preceding four races. Insist on 3–1 or less or two times as a *star marked favorite. Such a horse often goes long odds in today's race. The last race should be recent, but it doesn't have to be good. It also helps on this plan if the short odds races were at higher class than today's race.

More and more horse players are finding it tough to beat the races. I tried to keep up with the statistics and trends for over thirty years and definitely notice the increased burden of too many horses and horsemen in cutthroat competition. I find it much tougher to make a profit now than twenty years ago. I am a strict believer that *any* system is better than no system at all. The average player going to the track makes his race-to-race selection from a jumble of different rules and thoughts.

If you must play every race, here is a good little "trick system" that will beat disorganized play. Take the odds from the weight and play the highest figure. All you need is a program. Helter-skelter play will result in about a 15 percent or 20 percent flat play loss. This little odds-from-weight plan will just about break even and give you plenty of action. If you want to improve it further, it is necessary to buy a Racing Form and use a few more factors.

Still a very simple and fair rating plan goes like this: Add the odds last out to the finish po-

sition last out. Also add the number of days
since the last race to this figure. Then add in the
odds today, and take that accumulated total
from today's weight. This will always give you
a well-liked recently raced horse, and strangely
enough it will not always be the favorite by any
means. If you will get down to work on the wagering section of this book and handle your
money properly, you can grind out a gain by
any good system. Impatience and greed kill off
most system players.

Racing Tote Action Plans

At smaller tracks or in harness racing and dog
racing, this way of picking winners will usually
beat handicapping. The danger in picking plays
by totalizer betting action is finding too many
plays and trying to guess among them. Use some
organized rules governing your decisions. There
are three main types of active horses. Many systems have been devised around these three main
principles.

One good type of active horse generally more
overlooked than the other kinds is the "early
money" horse. This horse gets positive money
very early in the betting by persons not concerned with closing odds.

An early money active selection opens way
below his expected odds. It helps here if you do

not accept the Morning Line alone as a guide. A multiple consensus should also be consulted to get a better price estimate. The horse should open at 4–1 or less, and way below his estimated line. He should be the only horse in the race, at this time, doing this peculiar thing. Then, later in the betting, the horse should climb steadily in odds, confirming the out-of-proportion early action. If he confirms the early bet by doubling or almost doubling in odds, then he qualifies as a live horse, even if later he gets other types of action and comes down from his doubling figure.

The second type of live betting action horse is one that takes a sharp drop during the betting. If his odds cut 25 percent or more at one crack, be alerted! If this sudden drop is followed by a mild recovery, you can be sure that was a private lump sum of nonpublic money. If, however, a big drop occurs early in the betting, it doesn't always indicate anything unusual. Remember to look for the drop and mild recovery pattern. If a horse takes a big cut *late* in the betting, there is not only no time for a recovery as confirmation, but the public will usually jump on it and the horse will go down even further in a reactionary way. This latter type of "late droppers" is considered the most attractive by most people who have limited thinking about betting action.

The reactionary money just about destroys any profit potential in this late-dropping type.

The third type of betting action horse is based on an extreme underlay. This underlay should be unexplainable. For this reason you cannot take the line odds or program odds alone as a guide. Frequently the track odds maker will set his estimate too high. A giant consensus will indicate that much more public support is due. Therefore, you can't jump to conclusions on all underlays. Make sure it is of an unreasonable or unexplained nature. I like such an underlay to be 50 percent or more below the consolidated estimated price, and it should be the only such pronounced underlay in the race. Or, if not the only underlay, it should be the only one in the logical bracket, meaning the first three or four choices in closing odds.

Favorable tote action on a horse is similar to an added factor in the form, and it improves any system if used intelligently. Again I remind you that research and compilations guide you to the best rules of play to fit your personality and needs.

CASINO PLANS

If the hunch and luck players were to examine their own actions they would see that they are actually system players, but very crude ones. They are struggling to "get the message" or right hunch that will tell them when to increase their wagers or which way to go. These players make fun of nearby players with a definite plan but I think secretly they envy the person having nerve enough to try what everyone else says is impossible. They hate to show their own nonconformity or mental laziness and lack of planning.

Anyone who keeps track of the action soon learns that the system players *do* last longer and many *do* quit winners. They may give their profits back later by staying too long, but at least they put up a better fight. Gambling without a plan can soon become simple-minded and boring.

Dice Line Methods

The best methods with the smallest percentage bites are the dice *line* plays including *do* or *don't pass, do* or *don't come,* and odds on same. Know

in advance what you are going to do or are trying to accomplish. Your research and testing
should be completed and your capital should be
adequate *before* you tackle the tiger. Hold your
bets down or use a very conservative wagering
plan. When a good run develops, push the action
a bit stronger, but be ready to back off if it
fizzles out. Live to fight another day.

Bide your time. Don't panic and don't
plunge. Eventually the good swing will come
along. The only way to be in the right place at
the right time is to be in the right place all the
time. You have only −1.4 percent or less to
overcome, and you can lick it if you take a
long-range view.

If you do nothing else but become a "master
of the pendulum" you will be a winner. This is
what Nick the Greek and most of the big (some-
time) winners had going for them. They had the
patience, understanding, and stamina to wait out
the downswings and capitalize and quit ahead
on the upswings. Additionally they usually used
what you might call a "plateau" system of wagering. They didn't risk big amounts of their own
money. If luck was running bad, they would
back off or quit. If they got some distance ahead,
they would start playing for bigger and bigger
stakes.

The vast majority of the High Roller type of
dice players are "married" to the *pass line* and

come bets. Any table that isn't making points or passing is considered cold. The *pass line* is just as good as the *back line* and the *come* is just as good as the *don't come,* but it is limited thinking to catch only one kind of hot streak. A table can be going great for the *line* and *come* players when a *back line* run hits. I make money on either kind of run with my flexible patterns, and it is amazing to see how several "miss-outs" will clear a table of other players. There is nothing wrong with *pass* and *come* bets. You can specialize there and make money if you just give it thought and proper pendulum play or money management. Many good wagering plans are adaptable there, too.

The short-term gambler has a little better luck with a wagering plan than the long-term or full-time gambler. Remember, wagering plans are "living on borrowed time." If you use any sort of climb at all, it can hasten your reaching a break point or table limits; so, if you must use one, make it conservative.

The *pass only* player has much better organization to his wagering than the *pass* and *come* player. The *pass* and *come* player can invest anywhere from one unit to dozens between 7's. For this type of player only the "pendulum" makes a good wagering plan. He can improve it a little like this: Play one unit on all your bets when they are not clicking too well. Increase to

two for a while when it seems to click. If this
doesn't work out, back off to one. After about
ten attempts to get "off the ground," next increase your winning run hopefuls to three units.
Again back off if necessary and, when it starts
to click once more, rise to four for a while, and
so on. This is a mild form of "progression by series."

The *back line* or *don't pass* and the *don't come*
players are faced with the same problems of too
many bets. They, too, need to master the "pendulum" plan and learn to quit on their good
swings. A suggestion for *don't come* players is
to stop playing all the *don'ts* on every roll if the
7's are clicking or passes are succeeding too frequently. If a shooter gets any point and makes it
close in a few times, just put one unit on the
don't pass and wait it out. The *don't pass* and
laying of odds is a whisker better than *do pass*
and *taking odds because* you get more money
on the *free odds* lines. Therefore, the percentage
here is a bit better when you average the -1.4
bet with the odds money at zero percent. Since
there are many times more *front line* players
than *back line* players, there is a psychological
advantage in being a *back line* player. If you
believe the house is crooked or against the
majority of the players, you are on the preferred
side. Actually, the house gets an edge on either
side and there is no such thing as "with the

house." In fact, the house likes to equalize the board, just as a bookie is happiest when he has bets on all the horses in the race. His book is more in balance and he can't get clobbered by any lucky player. The gambling house and the bookie want favorable percentages, nothing else.

Owing to the disorganized, uncontrollable nature of *come* play, I prefer the *lines* only. They adapt nicely to pattern play and wagering plans. In fact, I rarely take or lay odds until I am out of debt. Remember, as in splitting pairs on a "21" game, if you are not sure you are in a winning run, you are only putting up more money. If you are a believer in pattern, as research will prove to you, it is also known that at times the *line* bets are much worse than −1.4 and at times they are much better, or on the plus side. Why, then, put up more money if the percentage is *not* leaning favorably?

I have had dice players look upon me with scorn when I fail to take odds, even as "21" players will get disgusted when you fail to split aces or double down on an 11. I let them feel smug and righteous and I don't hand it back to them when they go broke and I am still in the game. It wouldn't do any good, as they would still be convinced they played correctly and I was just lucky. To dice players, my recommendation is:

Open up your thinking and study cycle and pattern. Then with a little more favorable percentage and controllable game, go to work on money management.

Place Betting

Only the 6's and 8's are low-percentage *place* bets. A study of cycle here shows a pinch of flat play profit occurs after three 6's or three 8's come in a row or three of either before an intervening 7. Put up the six units and let your *place* bet ride until a 7 knocks it out. Do not put it up again until another similar sequence occurs. Note that, since it requires six units, this game takes quite a bit more capital than single-unit *line* play. If you mix the two on the same bankroll, you will be out of balance, overemphasizing the *place* game.

This *place* plan is just as adaptable to parlays or "pressing" your bets as any other method. The 7–6 odds are quite similar to even money. When you press the bet or let the profits ride, you draw off one unit of profit. I do not recommend *place* betting on the 4,5,9, or 10 at the larger negative percentage, no matter if one of those numbers gets hot. Remember, hot streaks can occur on *anything,* and only a fool chases all the rainbows.

Field Betting

This is usually a very bad bet unless you are in an area where they pay double on the 2 and triple on the 12. Then the negative percentage is reasonably small. The field can hit some pretty good runs. My research indicates that it should hit at least three in a row before it is considered mildly profitable or "warmed up." Even then the pinch of flat play profit is so small you have to parlay or triple your bet to compound the profit.

My "field system," then, goes like this: In proper field areas, if the field hits three times in a row, start with a one-unit bet. If it wins, let it ride. If that wins, let it ride again. In other words, shoot for a triple, paying 7–1. If you cash the 7–1, rack up 5 gain and put 2 back. This time just shoot for a parlay. Let the two ride until it becomes 8. If that parlay wins, again rack up a gain, and now come back for a three-unit bet which you again try to parlay. (See Profit Increaser type of wagering plan.) During a hot field run, the 2's and 12's will give you a thrilling added bonus. To capitalize this game, at least 300 units are suggested.

You can also use a gradual series pendulum sort of plan. Just remember, do not play the field on the Las Vegas Strip or any layout where you do not get all benefits.

Hardways and Any Craps

These are definitely *not* recommended, as cycling rarely overcomes the negative percentage. If you must indulge, do so lightly and try to play them only when they are "clicking." If an even point number has clicked two or three times in a row with no intervening seven, that is the most likely time for a *hardway* bet. If the craps numbers are running "hot," it is OK to try them for a short spell. But by all means back off when they cool down.

The best time to play craps or 11 is opposite the proper line bet only when craps or 11's are hot.

The best time to play a hardway number is when you have a larger back line bet against that number, and again only when the hardway number is in a favorable cycle.

Craps, 11's, or hardways should be played in much smaller proportions than the opposing line bets, or again you are out of balance, putting too much on the "insurance" type of poor percentage bet. The only advantage to such a bet is to keep the line game more stabilized.

Baccarat Plans

Every wagering method or pattern run that applies to even-money dice plans or roulette plans can be adapted to baccarat. There is a longshot play on baccarat, but it is a very bad percentage and I have no system suggestion for that. The main game in baccarat is purely a matter of pattern and money management. Like roulette, it has the advantage of being a sit-down game. Also, there is less confusion and you have a better chance to concentrate on your wagering. It is a very good and very beatable game even though we give it very little space in this book. In my compilations type of publications I have baccarat runs available to students of patterns.

Various "21" systems are not mentioned in this system section, because we covered that pretty well in the "21" chapter. The pendulum play, wagering plans, parlays, and all similar tactics are also adaptable to "21."

Roulette Systems

We could easily fill a thousand-page book with roulette systems. If there are fifty million Frenchmen, there are fifty million systems. There are so many different odds ranges and ways to play that lots of wagering possibilities are open. European roulette is a great game with a very small percentage bite. Given the same circumstances in America, I'm sure it would be my favorite game. I find it very beatable and very adaptable to cycle study.

I derive great joy and hobby entertainment from computerizing these good games on which voluminous records are available. For example, on one hundred thousand authentic roulette numbers I made a "gap book." Each number was tabulated in terms of the gap figure between hits. Then each split, each street, each four-block, each six-block, each dozen, each column, and each even money play was "gapped." This greatly condensed the big run of numbers and put the whole thing into a new perspective or dimension. Through this kind of work, one is able to learn the true value of patterns and to avoid being tricked by coincidence.

By plotting graphs from the totals of each approach, we can determine the peak of each cycle—when to get in and when to get out. Ridiculous, you say? They said that about the atomic bomb, television, and the airplane, too. I am not saying we know *exactly* when to pick up a number or group of numbers. What I am saying is that over the long-range period we can and *do* turn the percentage and improve cold selecting.

The reader will have to forgive me if I do not reveal all the findings of a life's work, but at least I have told how to find the same answers. The systems I give in this book are more than just "good ideas." The systems and ideas I pass along are intended as stepping stones to your success.

For my roulette game, I use an Eversharp pencil with an eraser. (A ball-point pen will let you down or smear at a critical time.) I use a little ruled card, folded down to very small hand size. I write down every number as it is spun. The red and black numbers are staggered off center in a vertical line. Thus I can immediately see a pattern that develops. I can also see the odd and even, high and low even-money patterns. I do not bother to keep special marks for the dozens or columns; they are rather obvious. The straight-up numbers that are getting "hot" are marked and followed in some instances.

Starting with the longest longshots (straight-up numbers at 35–1) you will find it much better to let the past results tell you which ones are hot rather than follow your favorite number or go to one that hasn't come in for a long time. When one hits *twice* within ten times, it is eligible for a very short time. If it hits *three* times within twenty, it can be followed a longer time. No matter what point you set, there are bound to be frustrations. For example, if you follow a number ten times, it can hit on the eleventh. Nevertheless you must set a rule, and research gives the best answers. I suggest: If it hits twice within ten, follow once or twice. If it hits three within twenty, follow up to ten times. If it hits within that ten, continue to follow ten times until the number cools off.

At this point I would like to discuss the fallacy of the so-called "biased wheel" theory. Much has been written about systems built on capitalizing on some wheel that seems to favor a certain number. It is claimed that the wheel is out of balance, or has a worn spot, or wider slot, or some reason for favoring a certain number, and the proof offered is a tabulation covering a day or two when that number predominated. The house is supposed to discover this oddity and change the wheel lest some college boys beat them for umpteen thousands.

Well, I have news for the wheel changers. I have yet to examine any group of numbers of up to ten thousand spins where some number *didn't* dominate. There was nothing abnormal about it and the wheel wasn't biased. Eventually that number played out or "cooled off." As a system student and games scientist, I am not impressed by hot runs. However I *do* know how to capitalize on them when they develop and I don't "flip" and think I have made the century's greatest discovery.

On the subjects of astrology, numerology, and extra-sensory perception (ESP), these, too, do not impress anyone who has examined hundreds of thousands of runs. When the ESP boys hit a hot streak they think it is their brain power at work. Actually the phenomenon would only be unusual if it didn't happen now and then. When someone plays a longshot and it clicks, he says something like, "I felt it coming." This is all well and good, but those players reach too much for those feelings. What happens is this: When you get a "hunch" and it proves correct, you get a big positive charge. This positive charge is much stronger than the negative discharge you get each time your hunch proves wrong. The end result is that you believe in your hunches.

There may be a wee bit of power in a true hunch but I couldn't say; I'm just a hard-headed Englishman and not gifted. However, I will match my researched cycle knowledge against hunches any day. I'm still in there playing, and the hunch players come and go by the thousands. The astrologers, numerologists, and ESP proponents aren't around very often or for long either.

I have talked to old-time roulette dealers and pointedly asked if they can control where the ball drops. Nearly all of the good ones can drop a ball on a specific side of a wheel. The expert ones can drop it within a quarter of a wheel. The good ones are about one in a hundred. The experts are one in a thousand. None claimed to be able to locate a ball in an exact number with but little more than a slight increase over the normal percentage. Does this mean you can forget the danger of an expert ball dropper? It does if you are not playing one or two straight-up numbers and nothing else. It can also be poison to a "sectional repeater" player.

The word of caution, then, is that you should avoid building your fortune on one specific number. If a young dealer is handling the wheel, you have nothing to fear in an honest and large casino. If the young one goes off shift and an older dealer comes on when someone is playing *one* number straight up, this is a time to be observing. You can really make the sweat stand out on this highly paid man's face if you now put a bet on a number on the opposite side of the wheel and, while you are at it, set one each in the other two quarters at equal intervals.

It isn't likely that you will ever encounter a magnetic wheel in a legal casino. I have played hundreds of wheels and have only seen one. The behavior of the ball is a dead giveaway. Normally it will tinkle and bounce when it comes down off the rim. When the "juice is on" it will slam into a slot. This type of pegging-in occurs occasionally by coincidence even without juice, so don't think you have found a magnetic wheel just because you see this happen. But if it happens frequently, and always opposite a big bet, it is time to take a walk.

Dice, too, have been magnetized. Again, it helps to be playing opposite the big money at a time like this. In large legal casinos this is about a one-in-ten-million chance, so forget it. Just like card advice to the country boy going to the city, "Don't play with strangers," confine your gambling to reliable places.

As the odds on roulette plays diminish, the profits of straight-run cycles also diminish. When you get down to the even-money shots, other patterns are more profitable than the straight (isolated) runs.

On split roulette numbers (17–1) the cycle is about half of the longer ones. They should hit three times within ten in order to follow five. Strips of three numbers in a row should hit three within eight to follow four times. Six blocks should hit three within five to be considered hot, then follow twice. Dozens or columns must hit three in a row to attract my action. Follow twice and then drop off. Even-money shots on isolated straight runs are fair at five, better at six. Follow one time only. All bets that win are continued on any warmed-up cycle.

Many roulette players have their favorite group of numbers. This is OK if you hold your bet down until they start clicking. The slumps can be a bit severe on any approach, and I think it is better to wait for a slump breaker. Good roulette players will increase their bets when clicking and walk away with a pile. Good roulette players *always* replace a winning bet.

If anything, you should increase it one unit or more after a winner. See wagering plans.

A very popular roulette system is to take two dozens or two columns on a steep progression. This is like a show bet paying 1–2. There is no percentage advantage in this system; it is strictly for short-term nervy players. If you want to improve it a bit, wait until your favorite two dozen has hit a few times and stop on each loser. The majority of systems for the games are founded on routine or normal losing-percentage selections. One should make an effort to break up the slumps and get onto favorable runs or profitable cycles. Then you are ready for advanced forms of money management.

SPECIAL WAGERING METHODS

Any effort to recover losses in a gambling session should be conservative. Otherwise, you will magnify them greatly. Once you are "even" with the game or a little ahead, you can abandon the conservatism and shoot for a glamorous gain if you like. To do this you need a definite plan. The "shoestring gambler" will let his bets ride and keep piling up. The trouble is, he has no set rule concerning when to break it off or extract a profit. One loser usually kills his entire dream.

Any player who stays at a table very long encounters at least one good run. Unfortunately most players lack the knowledge or nerve to take advantage of it. These people are the opposite extreme from the dreamer who blows the whole works trying to make a killing on a very small stake. With the plan I'm about to give you, it is possible to make a nice profit on any good run, a terrific profit on a prolonged run, and still not go broke when it breaks off.

To play the "profit increaser" plan it is necessary to deal in parlays or odds in excess of 1–1. All even-money bets are incomplete transactions until they win *two* in a row, paying 3–1. First,

144

remember, this profit increaser is not started until you are *out of debt*.

Your first parlay is started off at two units. If it loses, the *profit increaser* is dead. Go back to debt recovery until you are ahead again. If it *wins,* however, you are ready to start the climb. Your two units will become eight. Your next bet is always the *middle* stage of the preceding level. In other words, if you win the two it becomes four, then eight. Your next parlay starts off at four. If it loses, you still have a profit because your first parlay paid a profit of 6, you did not reinvest the entire amount.

If your first parlay won, 2 became 8; and if your second parlay won, 4 became 16. Now you go to the 8 level for the third parlay attempt. You are hoping that 8 becomes 16 and then 32. If it fails, you still have a reasonable profit. You made 2 on the first parlay, and reinvested 4. Since the second parlay was successful, you actually made 6 on your first parlay, you got your investment back. You did the same with your second parlay. At first you had a small gain but, after the parlay was completed, you could "lock up" some of the gain from the second parlay, too, and reinvest in the third.

Get a pencil and paper and you will see that your profits climb steadily as your bet size climbs. Any time it breaks off, you still have a nice profit. If, just *if* you happen to break into a prolonged good run and get by the third or fourth stage, the profits start to skyrocket. In a really good run you can get up to table limits and still have a profit in hundreds when the run breaks off. Of course, a player starting at a higher level, like a five-unit bet, will get to table limits quicker than one starting at two units. In fact, you should switch over to fives and tens somewhere along the line to keep from having to handle too many burdensome loose dollar chips. The game goes fast and you can't afford to be caught counting and miss a winner.

Once you have a reasonable profit in the "increaser" pile you can start taking or laying odds as well. This takes dexterity and practice. Gambling is a profession and you won't master it overnight.

My tabulations of straight runs on even-money patterns indicate that runs of 8 or more come up on an average of once every few hours. Runs of 10 or more come up about once a day. Runs of 14 or more come up about once a week. Runs in excess of 17 come up about once a month. Tie into one of the big ones some lucky time when you have no outstanding debt at its beginning and you can go out and buy that new car or whatever you want. This is a *definite* plan that works, not a dream. All you have to do is to learn to survive and put in the hours. About half of your good runs are wasted because at the time they come along you are involved in debt recovery. Also, not every player is able to put in many hours a day and not every player is capitalized to survive. So it isn't easy, but the gold is there.

Here is a special wagering plan you might like. I say you "might like" because I am hoping all speculation hopefuls *will* paper test and then cheap chip test plans before they go for big money. No plan is without its dangers and pitfalls. In the wagering chapter we skipped lightly over the "due column" method, noting that it climbed too steeply and tapped out too quickly. Here, now, are some excellent improvements on that basic idea.

We slow down the due column by shooting for less than full odds. For example, if you were trying to hit 3–1 shots, the due column would say to play one-third of the debt. One winner would then clean up the column. Instead of playing one-third, we play a constant one-tenth of the debt. Under this plan, your wagering will rise and fall and will always put more on the winners than on the losers. It is a good "grinder." It should turn the tide on any sensible selections.

The next improvement we add to our "less-than-full-odds" due column plan is a "take-out" of one unit per winner. When you subtract the profit from a winner from the total due, you take one less than the actual profit and put that one in your pocket or profit pile. Thus you are grinding out one unit profit per winner even though the due column is not down to base. For example, suppose your debt was 30. Your bet at 10 percent would be 3 units. If your winner paid 3–1, the 3 you invested would become 12, a profit of 9. Instead of taking 9 from the 30 debt, take 8 and put 1 into the profit "take-out." The new debt would be 22. The use of a take-out figure actually puts a little more than a 10 percent burden on your wagering plan, but you still use the simple and quick 10 percent calculating figure to arrive at your next bet.

With a little practice this entire plan can be kept in your head while at the table. If you lose count, all you have to do is recount your chips. A good player always knows in advance what his next bet will be, win or lose, and he is ready for either possibility. It takes practice to get fast at wagering in the proper place and wagering the proper amount but you must learn to do it.

For those with a really sharp money-handling skill, a further improvement on the "fixed percent due and take-out" plan is to use "multiple columns." When you get into multiple columns you can average a high column with a low one that just won out and got down to base. This gives you more "borrowed time" to get through a really bad downbeat. Multiple column takes a lot of pencil work and is all right on roulette or baccarat, but it is a bit clumsy for dice or black-jack. I prefer a single debt figure so I can quickly go over to the "profit increaser."

An average day in the life of Full-Time Gambler Holloway goes about like this: In the morning about thirty minutes are spent in a legal horse book. Careful spot plays are sought. Some days none appear. Betting on a definite plan is carried over from the previous day. After the calculations are made, I waste no time hanging around the book. Persons who sit in a horse book all day are like those going to the track, they wind up making too many dabble bets. You can make a nice living off the races if you control yourself and stick to careful selections.

There is no point in rushing to a casino and gambling around the clock. Visitors and com-pulsive gamblers play as if in a trance. Suddenly they wake up and their money is gone. The time to gamble is when all else is attended to and you are relaxed and composed. Gaming conditions are usually better in the afternoon and early eve-ning. After a winning session, call it a day and take advantage of the good food and shows available. Sometimes the daily profit can be made swiftly. Other times it can take hours and then you can gamble further into the evening. Actually it shouldn't be called gambling; treat it as strictly business. It helps to read a little list of reminder rules before you start the action. Make up your own rules from these chapters if you like.

Each player should be able to develop his own tailor-made winning procedures from plans outlined in this book. I personally consider authentic casino tabulations to be essential "tools of the trade." The reader can buy a Holloway Publications book entitled *Nevada Gaming Guide with Casino Compilations* for a fee of $20. These tabulations cover dice, roulette, keno, "21," and baccarat. They are equal to six months of steady play and would cost you a mint to compile. With this kind of research work you can test all your system ideas and wagering plans without spending a fortune in time and money. The author will also answer questions by correspondence. If interested in *Compilations* or further knowledge, you may write directly to: Louis G. Holloway, Box 5107, Las Vegas, Nevada 89111.

THE PSYCHOLOGICAL BATTLE

The toughest fight is not against percentage or finding a winning system. Acquiring the knowledge or the capital is not the hardest job. To win the main battle you have to master just one person—yourself.

If we were to try to sum up in one word why people lose at gaming, we would use the word, "miscalculation." This would first of all count miscalculation of the individual's own character. Complete understanding and self control are rare qualities.

Would you hand the keys of a high-powered automobile to a child who had had but one quick driving lesson and send him out into traffic and onto the freeways? You can't just read a list of instructions and then expect to react quickly and correctly under pressure and high-speed conditions. Any lesson that hasn't been practiced, studied, explained, and *made logical,* will not sink in very deeply. I'm not calling the readers of this book mere children in the field of speculation. I am saying that I see speculation infants at the tables all the time and it is up to you to avoid being one.

All around you and all through life you hear people say, "You can't beat the races," or "You can't beat the house." The fear of or belief in defeat is deeply planted. Churches and laws proclaim gambling an evil. Your parents probably told you that earning a living by any means other than honest toil was wrong. Thus, in the back of your mind there are mental blocks against making a living through speculation. The problem becomes one of brainwashing.

By now you should know speculation is a tough job, so we are not without toil. All business, politics, marriage, and life itself are gambles. So, if we play where it is legal, there is no moral issue.

Now for the big problem: You have to become a "believer." If you are still convinced that you "can't win," you will stay licked.

Many people going to a casino or race track are wise enough to know they haven't sufficient knowledge and do not take the game seriously. Their interest is in alleviating boredom. They don't want to work; all they want is a little luck. Perhaps some day they will get down to studying the game seriously, but it isn't likely because they are essentially "nonbelievers." They don't think it is worth the time and effort. This lack of faith reflects in their play and excuses away their foolish bets. Speculationwise, these are nice little children. Bless them, we need their money!

Another group of poor players may be called the "dropouts." These are the wise guys who think they know it all. They are not about to open their minds to further education. They play with bravado and try to show their contempt for money. Even when they win they are almost certain to give it all back trying to appear even bolder. Basically they are also "nonbelievers" in ultimate victory and all they ask is the favors of their goddess, Lady Luck, so they can look big for a while. The wise-guy type is only interested in his own image and isn't about to change any bad habits.

Next we have the type of players you could call "hangers-on." These have actually given up searching for the winning formula. They play with a defeatist attitude and should have left the scene long ago. Many leading psychiatrists claim the majority of gamblers really want to lose. I certainly don't agree with this theory. To me the majority are victims of greed. If they do get ahead, they want even more, and a downswing gets them while they are trying for a bigger gain.

Winning at gambling is like a prize fight in which you are up against a very tough old professional fighter. To beat him, you dare not make a mistake or he will clobber you. If you give him an opening, you deserve to get hit. Once you are on top you still have to fight correctly and just as hard or he will again take advantage of any slackening of effort on your part. In other words, speculation is a fighter's game.

If you hope to win, you have to have unlimited determination. You have to take your lumps, pick yourself up and try, try again. When you become a winner and you do better than other people, you will know why: Because you work hard and fight hard. Your type of work is constant training and discipline.

Race players would be better off if they were deaf or could turn off a hearing aid. In racing or gaming, if another player can influence your action and decisions, you aren't on very solid ground. No matter how smart he sounds or looks, he may just be on an upswing. The chances are that the other player hasn't put in the research time you have and doesn't know all the answers as well as you do. It is a strange thing that at a race track forty thousand losers can all be authorities.

At a casino, never envy the man with big money or a big pile of chips. You don't know how much he bought-in for or how rich he is out-side of his gambling life. You also don't know how much more he may have lost by that same method on previous occasions and you don't know if he will be able to increase the present pile by the same method he used to acquire it. Generally speaking, richer people play a looser game, as they have little regard for money.

Your mental balance is a very touchy thing. If temper creeps in, your efficiency falls off. Losses or victory can also give you a minor form of intoxication or even frenzy.

It is tough enough to stay on an even keel

without drink. If you add alcohol and think it doesn't affect your game, you didn't have a good game in the first place. You may think it sharpens your thinking to take just one drink. The drinks you get at a gaming table are stronger than the ones you buy at a bar, and for good reason. Your play gets looser and wilder; you take chances and break your rules. Drinking and social contacts should be separated from working hours.

It doesn't pay to get involved in conversations with others at the table. If you try to help them and show how smart you are, this little distraction can be just enough for your guard to drop, and the old pro socks you with a loser. If there are annoyances or distractions you can't ignore, it is better to get out of that game and take a break. There are plenty of break points in a game when you can hit the rest room or get a breath of fresh air.

Never play when hungry, sleepy, tired, or short of time. The constant fight to keep your personal control and think straight gets worse under the pressure of a losing streak. You don't need pep pills or energy boosters; you shouldn't be in the game under unsatisfactory conditions, so break it off. Finally, when you are winning and the pressure is off, you still have to keep from going wild and still have to follow a definite plan. The good gambler is cool and composed both when losing and when winning.

For a fitting close, here is a rule to guide you. This concerns the most important part: *when to quit*. The race tracks and casinos do not twist your arm and force you to come in or to continue playing. You can quit at any time, and this is one of your most powerful weapons. If you reach your stop-loss or run out of time and are forced to quit behind, this can be regarded merely as an intermission. The object of the game is to put up a good fight until you get ahead.

By all means don't be so relieved when you finally do get ahead that you quit too soon. In other words, *never quit in a winning streak or on a winner*. However, be ready to quit as soon as it breaks off. Let one or two losses come along and then quit before you give back all your gains. In capsule form, here is the rule and a symbol:

When you get ahead, quit on the downturn of an upswing.

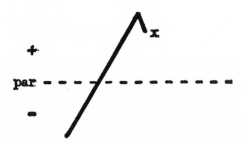

GOOD GAMING GUIDE RULES

+ Never make a bad percentage play.
+ Speculate only in large, legal, reputable establishments.
+ Play only under completely satisfactory conditions.
+ Ignore distractions, drinks, and other people's luck.
+ Base play on a thoroughly researched, well-understood plan.
+ Make sure your capitalization is adequate to wagering size and scale.
+ Beware of greed in overbetting, plunging, or staying too long.
+ Set a loss limit.
+ Don't use credit or write checks.
+ Have patience with losing periods; push luck only in winning ones.
+ Quit on the downturn after an upswing.

INDEX

159